The Pilgrim's Progress Primer

By Mary Godolphin & William C. Nichols

With Illustrations by H. C. Selous & M. Paolo Priolo
Colorized by Serena Scholl,
Daria Danielson, and Robin Nichols

International Outreach, Inc.
P.O. Box 1286, Ames, Iowa 50014

This book is dedicated to my family: To my wife Robin, who spent many, many hours coloring drawings, and to my children, Ian and Hannah, who helped me to view this project through the eyes of a child.

Scripture quotes in the footnotes are from the King James Version of the Holy Bible. References to scripture passages in the text are references only and do not quote directly from the scriptures due to the necessity that words in the text be one syllable in length.

Front cover etching by H. C. Selous colorized by Robin Nichols
Back cover etching by M. Paolo Priolo colorized by Serena Scholl
Cover layout courtesy of Steve Erb of Nite Owl Printing, Ames, Iowa

International Outreach, Inc.
P. O. Box 1286, Ames, Iowa 50014
http://members.aol.com/intoutreach/pricelist.html
http://members.aol.com/intoutreach/NarrowWay.html

The Pilgrim's Progress was written by John Bunyan in Bedford prison where he had been confined for preaching the gospel of Jesus Christ as a Dissenter. It was first published in 1679 and, next to the Bible, it is the most widely read book in history. Yet many in today's generation, even among Christians, have never read it.

It was one to two years ago when I was asked by a friend to consider publishing a children's version of *Pilgrim's Progress*. He had several versions of the book including one published in the 1800's in which all the words were one syllable in length with the exception of proper names and place names. This version, written by Mary Godolphin, became the foundation on which this current volume was built. At the same time I purchased another work from the 1800's which contained the most beautiful etchings I had ever seen in any version of *Pilgrim's Progress*.

As I considered the project, it became my intent to combine the best of the two versions into one volume. Mary Godolphin had greatly abbreviated the original work. I began by starting to edit her version and also added sections to her work as I went along. The result is what you have before you. The text is nearly twice the length of the original work by Mary Godolphin. The original etchings done by H. C. Selous and M. Paolo Priolo have been colorized by Serena Scholl, Daria Danielson, and my wife Robin. Many hundreds of hours have gone into the colorization process, so that the beauty of the original etchings would be preserved and that they would be attractive to today's readers. I would like to thank Serena, Daria, and Robin for their excellent work in adding to the beauty of these etchings. I would also like to thank the people at the Iowa State University Printing Service for their work in scanning the original etchings. Our children, Ian and Hannah, have also aided me in helping me to see this project through the eyes of a child.

The names of persons (Chris-tian, Ig-no-rance, etc.) and places (The Ci-ty of De-struc-tion, Van-i-ty Fair, etc.) have been hyphenated as they were in Mary Godolphin's version. Footnotes have been added to help explain more about the characters who meet Christian in his journey to The Celestial City. These footnotes are primarily written for adults to assist them in explaining to their children more about the characters. In cases where it is relatively easy to understand who the characters are and what they represent, no footnote is added (Hopeful, Know-ledge, Sin-cere, etc.). In the case of the maidens who greet Christian at the Palace Beautiful, dictionary definitions of their names were used. Other more complex characters (Talk-a-tive, By-Ends, etc.) are dealt with in more detail. I urge you not to ignore the footnotes, but to reflect upon them. I believe they will help in understanding the deeper meaning of Bunyan's work.

My intent in publishing this edition of *Pilgrim's Progress* is to help introduce John Bunyan's incomparable work to a generation (both children and adults) who have never read the original. Bunyan saw with much clearer eyes than most see today. His representations through his characters of those who are headed for the Celestial City having not come in through the Wicket Gate are brilliant sketches of those we see all around us today, inhabiting our church pews, sitting on our elder boards, and sometimes even preaching from our pulpits. It is my prayer that God will bless this work and make it an instrument through which some may find entrance into The Celestial City, instead of being like Bunyan's character Ignorance, who with delusions of heaven in their minds, are turned away at the last moment and taken to the door in the side of the hill.

William C. Nichols
Ames, Iowa
September 13, 1999

THE PILGRIM'S PROGRESS
IN THE SIMILITUDE OF A DREAM

KNOCK AND IT SHALL BE OPENED

As I went through the wild waste of this world, I came to a place where there was a den, and I lay down in it to sleep. While I slept, I dreamed a dream, and lo! I saw a man whose clothes were in rags, and he stood with his face from his own house, with a book in his hand, and a great load on his back.

I saw him read from the leaves of a book, and as he read he wept and shook with fear; and at length he broke out with a loud cry, and said, What shall I do?

So in this plight he went home, and as long as he could he held his peace, so that his wife and young ones should not see his grief. But at length he told them his mind, and thus he spoke, O my dear wife, and you my young ones, I, your dear friend, am full of woe, for a load lies hard on me; and more than this, I have been told that our town will be burnt with fire from Hea-ven, in which I, you my wife, and you my sweet young ones, shall be lost, if means be not found to save us.

This sad tale struck all who heard him with awe, not that they thought what he said to them was true, but that they had fears that some weight must be on his mind; so, as night now drew near, they were in hopes that sleep might soothe his brain, and with all haste they got him to bed. But the night was as bad to him as the day, for he spent it in sighs and tears, and not in sleep.

When the morn broke, they sought to know how he did. He told them, Worse and worse; and he set to talk once more in the same strain as he had done; but they took no heed of it. By and by, to drive off his fit, they spoke harsh words to him; at times they would laugh, at times they would chide, and some times they would take no note of him. So he went to his room to pray for them, as well as to nurse his own grief. He would go, too, in the fields to read and pray, and thus for some days he spent his time.

Now I saw in my dream that one day, as he did walk in the fields with his book in his hand, he gave a groan—for he felt as if a dark cloud were on his soul—and he burst out as he was wont to do, and said, What shall I do to save my soul?

I saw, too, that he gave wild looks this way and that, as if he would run; yet he stood still, for he could not tell which way to go. As last, a man whose name was E-van-gel-ist* came up to him and said, Why do you weep?

---

* Evangelist warns sinners to flee from the certain judgment of God's wrath to come. He represents one who gives the message of salvation in Jesus Christ to sinners and guides them in their journey along the Way to the Celestial City.

EVANGELIST DIRECTS CHRISTIAN TO THE WICKET GATE

He said, Sir, I see by this book in my hand that I am to die, and that then God will judge me. Now I dread to die.

E-VAN-GEL-IST. Why do you fear to die, since this life is so full of grim and dark days?

The man said, I fear that this load on my back will sink me down to the grave, and I shall fall down to Hell. Sir, if I be not fit for the jail, I am not fit to meet the Judge, nor that to which He will doom me, and the thoughts of these things make me cry.

If this be your case, said E-van-gel-ist, why do you stand still?

But the man said, I know not where to go.

Then he gave him a scroll with these words on it, Flee from the wrath to come.

3

When the man read it he said, Which way must I flee?

E-van-gel-ist held out his hand to point to a Gate in a wide field, and said, Do you see the Wick-et Gate?

The man said, No.

Do you see that bright light?

He then said, I think I do.

Keep that light in your eye, said E-van-gel-ist, and go straight up to it; so shall you see the Gate, at which, when you knock, it shall be told you what you are to do.

Then I saw in my dream that Chris-tian—for that was his name—set off to run. Now he had not gone far from his own door, when his wife and young ones, who saw him, gave a loud wail to beg of him to come back; but the man put his hands to his ears, and ran on with a cry of, Life! Life! Life that shall not end! So he did not look back, but fled to the midst of the plain.

The friends of his wife, too, came out to see him run, and as he went, some were heard to mock him, some to use threats, and there were two who set off to fetch him back by force, the names of whom were Ob-sti-nate* and Pli-a-ble.* Now, by this time, the man had gone a good way off, but at last they came up to him.

Then said Chris-tian, Friends, why are you come?

To urge you to go back with us, they said.

But he said, That can by no means be; you dwell in The Ci-ty of De-struc-tion, the place where I, too, was born. And if you die there, you will sink down to a place which burns with fire; be wise, good friends, and come with me.

What! said Ob-sti-nate, and leave our friends, joys, and goods back there?

Yes, said Christ-tian, for all that which you might leave is but a grain to that which I seek, and if you will go with me and hold it firm, you shall fare as well as I; for there, where I go, you will

---

* Obstinate does not believe the Word of God and is against those who do. He is stubborn and proud, and wants all people to agree with him in everything.

* Pliable is easily persuaded to seek that which sounds good to him, but is not willing to endure any hardship or difficulty to get it. He is like those who came out of Egypt who at first "sang his praise," but "soon forgat his works" and then "provoked him to anger" by their actions (Psalm 106:12, 13, 29). Pliable's interest in the Kingdom of God arises purely from self-love and what he can gain for himself, not from any genuine interest in or love to God.

CHRISTIAN SETTING OUT FROM THE CITY OF DESTRUCTION

find all you want and more to spare. Come with me and prove my words.

OB-STI-NATE. What are the things you seek, since you leave all the world to find them?

CHRIS-TIAN. I seek those joys that fade not, which are laid up in Hea-ven—safe there for those who go in search of them. Read it so, if you will, in my book.

OB-STI-NATE. Tush! Off with your book. Will you go back with us or not?

CHRIS-TIAN. No, not I, for I have laid my hand to the plow.

OB-STI-NATE. Come, friend Pli-a-ble, let us turn back and leave him; there is a troop of such mad, vain fools who, when they take up with a whim by the end, are more wise in their own eyes than ten men of good sound sense, who know how to think.

PLI-A-BLE. Nay, do not scorn him; if what the good Christian says is true, the things he looks to are of more worth than ours: my heart moves me to go with him.

OB-STI-NATE. What! more fools still! Go back with me, go back, and be wise.

CHRIS-TIAN. Nay, but do you come with me, Pli-a-ble; there are such things to be had as those I just spoke of, and more, too. If you give no heed to me, read here in this book which comes to us from God, and proves the truth of it all.

PLI-A-BLE. Well, friend Ob-sti-nate, I think now I have come to a point; and I mean to go with this good man, and to cast my lot in with his. Then he said to Chris-tian, Do you know the way to the place you speak of?

CHRIS-TIAN. I am told by a man whose name is E-van-gel-ist, to do my best to reach a small Gate that is in front of us, where I shall be told how to find the Way.

So they went on side by side.

OB-STI-NATE. And I will go back to my place; I will not be one of such vain folk like you.

Now I saw in my dream, that when Ob-sti-nate was gone back, Chris-tian and Pli-a-ble set off to cross the plain, and they spoke thus as they went:

CHRIS-TIAN. Well, Pli-a-ble, how do you do now? I am glad you have a mind to go with me.

6

PLI-A-BLE. Come, friend Chris-tian, since there are none but we two here, tell me more what the things are, and of the joy we shall have in them, in that place to where we go?

CHRIS-TIAN. I can find them in my heart, though I know not how to speak of them with my tongue; but yet, since you wish to know, this book tells us we are to dwell with a King whose realm has no ends, and there we shall live as long as He lives.

PLI-A-BLE. Well said, and what else?

CHRIS-TIAN. That there are crowns of gold in store for us, and robes that will make us shine like the sun.

PLI-A-BLE. This is quite good; and what else?

CHRIS-TIAN. That there shall be no more care, nor grief, nor pain; for He that owns the place will wipe all tears from our eyes.

PLI-A-BLE. And what friends shall we find there?

CHRIS-TIAN. There we shall be with Ser-a-phims and Che-ru-bims, and it will daze your eyes to look on them, and all the saints will be there in crowns of gold. There we shall meet those who in this world have stood out for the faith, and have been burnt at the stake, and thrown to wild beasts, for the love they bore to the Lord. They will not harm us, but will greet us with love, for they will walk in the sight of God.

PLI-A-BLE. But how shall we get to share all this?

CHRIS-TIAN. The Lord of that land says, if we do with all our hearts wish to gain that world, we shall be free to have it.

PLI-A-BLE. Well, my good friend, glad am I to hear of these things: come on, let us mend our pace.

CHRIS-TIAN. I can not go so fast as I would, 'cause of this load on my back.

Then I saw in my dream that just as they had come to an end of this talk, they drew near to a Slough of mire that was in the midst of the plain, as they took no heed, they both fell in the bog. The name of the Slough was De-spond. Here they lay for a time in the mud, and the load that Chris-tian had on his back made him sink all the more in the mire.

PLI-A-BLE. Ah! friend Chris-tian, where are you now?

CHRIS-TIAN. In truth, I do not know.

Then Pli-a-ble got in a rage and said to his friend, Is this the bliss of which you told me all this while? If we have such ill speed when we first set out, what may we look for 'twixt this and the end of our Way? You shall have the brave land, but not with me, and then he gave a lunge or two, and got out of the mire on that side of the Slough which was next to his own house; then off he went, and Chris-tian saw him no more.

So Chris-tian was left to twist and turn in the Slough of De-spond as well as he could; yet his aim was to reach that side of the Slough that was next to the Gate, which at last he did, but he could not get out 'cause of the load that was on his back; till I saw in my dream that a man came to him whose name was Help, who did ask him, What do you do here?

CHRIS-TIAN. I was sent this way by a man named E-van-gel-ist, who told me to pass up to The Wick-et Gate, that I might flee from the wrath to come; and on my way to it, I fell in here.

HELP. But why did you not look for the steps?

CHRIS-TIAN. Fear came so hard on me that I fled the next way and fell in.

Then said Help, Give me your hand. So he gave him his hand, and he drew him out, and set him on firm ground, and told him to go on his Way.

Then in my dream I went up to Help and said to him, Sir, since this place is on the Way from The Ci-ty of De-struc-tion to The Wick-et Gate, how is it that no one mends this path of ground, so that those who come by may not fall in the Slough? HELP. This Slough is such a place as no one can mend. It is the spot to which does run the scum and filth that come with proof of the guilt of sin, and that is why it is known as the Slough of De-spond. When the man of sin wakes up to a sense of his own lost state, doubts and fears rise up in his soul, and all of them drain down and sink in this place: and it is this that makes the ground so bad. True there are good and sound steps in the midst of the Slough, but at times it is hard to see them; or if they can be seen, men's heads are so dull that they step to one side, and fall in the mire. But the ground is good when they have once got in at the Gate.

Now I saw in my dream that by this time Pli-a-ble had gone back to his house once more, and that his friends came to see him; some said how wise he was to come home, and some that he was a fool to have gone. Some, too, were found to make sport of his lack of spine, and they said, Well, had I set out, I would not have been so base as to come back for a Slough in the road.

HELP DRAWS CHRISTIAN OUT OF THE SLOUGH OF DESPOND

So Pli-a-ble was left to sneak off; but at last he got more heart, and then all were heard to turn their taunts, and laugh at poor Chris-tian. Thus much for Pli-a-ble.

Now as Chris-tian went on his Way, he saw a man come through the field to meet him, whose name as Mr. World-ly Wise-man*, and he dwelt in the town of Car-nal Pol-i-cy, which was near that whence Chris-tian came. He had heard some news of Chris-tian; for his flight from the Ci-ty of De-struc-tion had made much noise, and was now the talk far and near. So he said, How now, good sir, where do you go with such a load on your back?

CHRIS-TIAN. In truth, it is a great load; and if you ask me where I go, I tell you, Sir, I must go the The Wick-et Gate in front of me, for there I shall be put in a Way to get rid of my great load.

WORLD-LY WISE-MAN. Have you not a wife and young ones?

CHRIS-TIAN. Yes, but with this load I do not seem to take joy in them as I did; and, in truth, I feel as if I had none.

WORLD-LY WISE-MAN. Will you hear me if I lay out a good plan for you?

CHRIS-TIAN. If what you say be good, I will, for I stand much in need of help.

WORLD-LY WISE-MAN. I would urge you then, with all speed, to get rid of your great load; for your mind will not be at rest till then.

CHRIS-TIAN. That is just what I seek to do. But to get it off my self, I can not and there is no man in our land who can take it off of me; so I shall go on this Way, as I told you, that I may be rid of it.

WORLD-LY WISE-MAN. Who told you come this way to be rid of it?

CHRIS-TIAN. One that I took to be a wise and good man; his name is E-van-gel-ist.

---

* Worldly Wiseman is a man who is wise in the ways of the world, but not the ways of God. He believes that one can find God through living a good life and doing their best to keep the Ten Commandments. He is filled with self-righteousness. The humbling way of the cross and a life of self-denial for Christ are foolishness to him, for he values ease, pleasure, and being well thought of by men.

WORLD-LY WISE-MAN. Hark at what I say: there is not a worse way in the world than that on which he has sent you, and that you will find if you take him for your guide. In this short time you have met with bad luck, for I see the mud of the Slough of De-spond is on your clothes. Hear me, for I have seen more of the world than you: in the way you go, you will meet with pain, woe, thirst, lack of food, wild beasts, the sword, too— in a word, death! Why should you seek to bring these things on to you? Take no heed of what E-van-gel-ist tells you.

CHRIS-TIAN. Why, sir, this load on my back is worse to me than all those things of which you speak; nay, I care not what I meet with in the Way, if I can but get rid of my load.

WORLD-LY WISE-MAN. How did you come by your load?

CHRIS-TIAN. By what I read out of this book in my hand.

WORLD-LY WISE-MAN. I thought so; and like more weak men I know, who aim at things too high for them, you have lost heart, and run in the dark at great risk, to gain you know not what.

CHRIS-TIAN. I know what I would gain; it is ease from my great load.

WORLD-LY WISE-MAN. But why will you seek for ease thus, when I could put you in the way to gain it where there would be no risk? The cure is at hand; in place of loss of life and limb you shall meet with peace, friends, and a safe trip.

CHRIS-TIAN. Pray, sir, tell me of your good plan.

WORLD-LY WISE-MAN. Well, in yon town, which you can see from here—the name of which is Mor-al-i-ty—there dwells a man whose name is Le-gal-i-ty, a wise man and a man of some rank, who has skill to help men off with such loads as yours from their backs. I know he has done a great deal of good in that way: Ay, and he has the skill to cure those who, from the loads they bear, are not quite sound in their wits. To him, as I said, you may go and get help. His house is but a mile from this place, and should he not be at home, he has a son whose name is Ci-vil-i-ty, who can do it just as well. There, I say, you may go to get rid of your load. I would not have you go back to your old home, but you can send for your wife and young ones, and you will find that food there is cheap and good and what will please you best is, there you shall live by good friends, and be well thought of.

So at last Chris-tian made up his mind. If this be true it is the best thing I can do. So he said, Sir, which is the way to this good man's house?

WORLD-LY WISE-MAN. Do you see that high hill?

CHRIS-TIAN. Yes, I do.

WORLD-LY WISE-MAN. By that hill you must go, and the first house you come to is his.

So Chris-tian did turn out of his Way to find Le-gal-i-ty's house to seek for help. But, lo, when he had got close up to the hill, it was so steep and high that he had fears lest it should fall on his head; so he stood still, as he knew not what to do. His load, too, grew more hard to bear than when he was on the

right road. Then came flames of fire out of the hill, that made him quake for fear lest he should be burned.

And now it was a great grief to him that he had lent his ear to World-ly Wise-man and it was well that he just then saw E-van-gel-ist come to meet him; though at the sight of him he felt a deep blush creep on his face for shame. So E-van-gel-ist drew near, and when he came up to him, he gazed at him with a fierce stare and said, What do you do here, Chris-tian?

To these words Chris-tian knew not what to say, so he stood quite mute. Then E-van-gel-ist went on thus: Are you not the man that I saw weep near The Ci-ty of De-struc-tion?

CHRIS-TIAN. Yes, dear sir, I am the man.

E-VAN-GEL-IST. Did not I point out to you the Way to the Wick-et Gate?

CHRIS-TIAN. Yes, you did, sir.

E-VAN-GEL-IST. How is it, then, that you have so soon gone out of the Way?

CHRIS-TIAN. When I had got out of the Slough of De-spond I met a man who told me that in a town near, I might find one who could take off my load.

E-VAN-GEL-IST. What was he?

CHRIS-TIAN. He had fair looks, and said much to me, and at last got me to yield; so I came here. But when I saw this hill, and how it hangs o'er the path, I made a stand, lest it should fall on my head.

E-VAN-GEL-IST. What said the man to you?

When E-van-gel-ist had heard from Chris-tian all that took place, he said, Stand still that I may show thee the words of God: See that ye turn not from Him that speaks, for if we turn from Him that speaks from Hea-ven, how shall we not feel His wrath? Then E-van-gel-ist went on to read, Now the just shall live by faith; but if a man draw back, my soul shall have no joy in him. Is not this the case with you? he said. Have you not drawn back your feet from the Way of peace, so that you are at risk to fall in to Hell? Do you not spurn the Most High God?

Then Chris-tian fell down at his feet as dead, and said, Woe is me, for I am filled with sin!

At the sight of which, E-van-gel-ist caught him by the right hand, and said, All manner of sin shall be washed clean. Be a man with faith, and hope it will be so with you.

Then did Chris-tian find some strength, and stood up.

E-VAN-GEL-IST. I pray you give more heed to the things that I shall tell you of. The Lord says, Strive to go in at the Strait Gate, the Gate to which I send you, for strait is the Gate that leads to life, and few there be that find it. Why did you set at nought the words of God, for the sake of a World-ly Wise-man? That is, in truth, the right name for such as he. The Lord hath told thee that he who will save his life, shall lose it. He to whom you were sent for ease, Le-gal-ity by name, could not set you free; no man yet has got rid of his load through him; he could but show you the way to woe, for by the deeds of the law no man can be rid of his load. So that World-ly Wise-man and his friend Le-gal-ity are false guides; and as for his son Ci-vil-ity, he is a fraud and can not help you.

Now Chris-tian, in great dread, could think of not a thing but death, and sent forth a sad cry in grief that he had gone from the right Way. Then he spoke once more to E-van-gel-ist in these words: Sir, what think you? Is there hope? May I now go back, and strive to reach The Wick-et Gate? I grieve that I gave ear to this man's voice; but may my sin find grace?

E-VAN-GEL-IST. Thy sin is quite great, for you have gone from the Way that is good to tread in false paths, yet the man at the Gate will let you in, for he has good will for men; but take heed that you turn not to the right hand nor to the left, lest God's wrath come on you.

Then did Chris-tian make a move to go back, and E-van-gel-ist gave him a kiss and a smile, and wished him God Speed.

So he went on with haste, nor did he speak on the road; and could by no means feel safe till he was on the path which he had left. In time, he got up to the Gate. Now o'er the top of the Gate he read words which said those who would knock could go in, so he gave more than two or three knocks, and said, May I go in here?

At last there came a grave man to the Gate, whose name was Good-will, and he said, Who is there? Where do come you from and what would you have?

CHRIS-TIAN. I come from The Ci-ty of De-struc-tion with a load of sins on my back; but I am on my way to Mount Zi-on, that I may be set free from the wrath to come; and as I have

CHRISTIAN AT THE WICKET GATE

been told that the Way is through this Gate, I would know, Sir, if you will let me in?

GOOD-WILL. With all my heart.

So he flung back the Gate. But just as Chris-tian went in he gave him a pull. Then said Chris-tian: What means that? Good-will told him that a short way from this Gate there was a strong fort, of which Be-el-ze-bub was the chief, and that from there he and the rest that dwelt there shot darts at those that came up to the Gate to try to kill them ere they got in.

Then said Chris-tian: I come in with joy and with fear. So when he had gone in, the man at the Gate said: Who sent you here?

CHRIS-TIAN. E-van-gel-ist told me to come and knock (as I did); and he said that you, Sir, would tell me what I must do.

GOOD-WILL. The door is thrown back wide for you to come in.

CHRIS-TIAN. Now I seem to reap the good of all the risks I have met with on the Way.

GOOD-WILL. But how is it that no one comes with you?

CHRIS-TIAN. None of my friends saw that there was cause of fear, as I did.

GOOD-WILL. Did they know of your flight?

CHRIS-TIAN. Yes, my wife and young ones saw me go, and I heard their cries as they ran out to try and stop me. Some of my friends, too, would have had me come home, but I put my hands o'er my ears, and so came on my Way.

GOOD-WILL. But did none of them come out to beg of you to go back?

CHRIS-TIAN. Yes, both Ob-sti-nate and Pli-a-ble came, but when they found that I would not yield, Ob-sti-nate did rant and rail and went home, but Pli-a-ble came with me as far as the Slough of De-spond.

GOOD-WILL. Why did he not come through it?

When Chris-tian told him the rest, he said: Ah, poor man! Is the bliss of Hea-ven such a small thing to him, that he did not think it worth while to run a few risks to gain it?

Sir, said Chris-tian, there is not much to choose twixt him and me. Then he told Good-will how he had been led from the straight path by Mr. World-ly Wise-man.

GOOD-WILL. Oh, did he light on you? What? He would have had you seek for ease at the hands of Mr. Le-gal-i-ty. They are, in truth, both of them cheats. And did you take heed of what he said?

So Chris-tian told him all and then said, It was God's grace that E-van-gel-ist came to me, else I had not come here. But now that I am come, said he, I am more fit for death, than to stand and talk to my Lord. But oh, the joy it is to me to be here!

GOOD-WILL. We keep none out that knock at this Gate, let them have done what they may ere they came here; for they are in no wise cast out. So, good Chris-tian, come with me, and I will teach you the way you must go. Look in front of you. Do you see this Nar-row Way? That is the Way which was laid down by Christ and the wise men of old, and it is as straight as a rule can make it. This is the Way you must go.

CHRIS-TIAN. But is there no turn or bend by which one who knows not the road might lose his way?

GOOD-WILL. Yes, there are quite a few such paths that butt down on this Nar-row Way, and these paths are wide; yet by this you may judge the right from the wrong—the right are straight and are by no means wide.

Then I saw in my dream that Chris-tian said, Could you not help me off with his load on my back?—for as yet he had not got rid of it. He was told, As to your load, you must bear it till you come to the place of De-liv-er-ance, for there it will fall from your back on its own.

Then Chris-tian would have set off on the road; but Good-will said, After you have gone a ways from the Gate, you will come to the house of the In-ter-pre-ter*, at whose door you must knock, and he will show you good things. Then Chris-tian took leave of his friend, who bade him God Speed.

He now went on till he came to the house of the In-ter-pre-ter, where he did knock, and knock, and knock. At last one came to the door and said, Who is there?

CHRIS-TIAN. I have come to see the good man of the house.

So in a short time In-ter-pre-ter came to him and said, What would you have?

CHRIS-TIAN. Sir, I am come from the Ci-ty of De-struc-tion, and am on my way to Mount Zi-on. I was told by the man that stands at the Wick-et Gate, that if I came here you would show me good things that would help me.

Then In-ter-pre-ter did ask a man to bring a light and he took Chris-tian to a room, and there he saw on the wall the print of one who had a grave face, whose eyes were cast up to Hea-ven, and the Best of Books was in His hand, the Law of Truth was on His lips, and the world was at his back. He stood

---

* The Interpreter, whose ministry seems to parallel that of the Holy Spirit in being a Counselor, Helper, and Guide, teaches Christian truths which will aid him in his journey. Among the things Christian learns are how the law stirs up sin, the importance of patience in waiting for eternal rewards rather than living for the pleasures of sin now, the necessity of striving to enter the Narrow door, the danger of spiritual slothfulness, and the importance of being ready for the final judgment.

INTERPRETER.SHOWS.CHRISTIAN.THE.ROOM.FULL.OF.DUST

as if He would plead for men, and a crown of gold hung near His head.

CHRIS-TIAN. What does this mean?

IN-TER-PRE-TER. I have shown you this print first, for this is He who is to be your sole guide when you can not find your Way to the land to which you go; so take good heed to what I have shown you, lest you meet with some who say that they would lead you in the right Way; but their way goes down to death.

Then he took him to a large room that was full of dust, for it had not been swept since it was made; and In-ter-pre-ter told a man to sweep it. Now when he did so, such clouds of dust flew up, that it made Chris-tian choke. Then said In-ter-pre-ter to a maid that stood by, Make the floor moist that the dust may not rise; and when she had done this, it was swept with ease.

Then said Chris-tian, What means this?

IN-TER-PRE-TER. This room is the heart of that man who knows not the grace of God. The dust is his in born sin and the vice that is in him that makes him foul. He that swept first is the Law, but she who made the floor moist is The Gos-pel. Now as soon as you saw the first of these sweep, the dust did so fly that you did choak, and the room could not be made clean by him; this is to show you that the Law as it works does not cleanse the heart from sin, but gives strength to sin, so as to rouse it up in the soul. Then you next saw the maid come in to lay the dust; so is sin laid low and the soul made clean by faith in The Gos-pel.

I saw in my dream that the In-ter-pre-ter led him by the hand to a room where sat two small boys, each in his chair. Their names were Pas-sion* and Pa-tience*. Pas-sion was ill at ease, but Pa-tience was quite calm. Then said Chris-tian, Why is Pas-sion so ill at ease? The In-ter-pre-ter said, Their lord would have him wait for his best things till the first of next year, but he would have all now; but Pa-tience knows how to wait.

Then one brought Pas-sion a bag of gold coins, and spread them out at his feet. Pas-sion took them up with joy and a laugh of scorn for Pa-tience. But I saw that in a short time he did waste them, and all he had left was rags.

Then said Chris-tian, Make this more clear to me.

IN-TER-PRE-TER. These lads are two types: Pas-sion of the men of this world, and Pa-tience of the men of that which is to come. For, as you saw, Pas-sion will have all now, that is, in this world, so the men of this world must have all their good things now. They can not wait till next year, that is, till the next

---

* Passion is like the Prodigal Son who will have all his good things now so that he might spend them upon the pleasures and lusts of the flesh. And like the Prodigal he wastes all and is left in rags. He indulges himself in a selfish lifestyle, living only to please himself. What he sees now is of much more value to him than the things of eternity, which cannot be seen.

* Patience represents those who walk by faith and not by sight. Patience has his eye on eternity and is not drawn aside to follow after the temptations of the world. He sows his seed now and waits for his harvest in the future, when he will be rewarded in the world to come.

CHRISTIAN IS SHEWN THE PARABLE OF THE PASSION AND PATIENCE.

world, for their share of good. That old word, A bird in the hand is worth two in the bush, is of more weight with them than all God's Word says of the good of the world to come.

But as Pas-sion soon did waste them, and had not a thing left but rags, so will it be with all such men at the end of this world. So Pas-sion, who had his good things first, has not so much cause to laugh at Pa-tience, as Pa-tience, who had his best things last, will have to laugh at Pas-sion.

First must give place to last, since last must have his time to come; but last does not have to give place at all, for there is no more to come. He, then, who has his part first, must have a time in which to spend it; but he who has his part last, will have it as long as God shall live.

Then I see, said Chris-tian, it is not best to wish for things that now are, but wait for things which are to come.

IN-TER-PRE-TER. You say truth; for the things that are seen are for a brief time, but the things that are not seen are for the life which shall have no end.

Then I saw in my dream that In-ter-pre-ter led Chris-tian to a place where there was a fire by a wall, and one stood by it and all the time wet it to quench it, yet the flame rose more high and hot. This fire, said the In-ter-pre-ter, is the work of grace in the heart; he that wets it to put it out is the Dev-il; but you shall see why the fire burns more high and hot in spite of him. So he took him to the back of the wall, where he saw a man with a jar in his hand, from which he did pour oil on the fire all the time, but out of sight. This is Christ, said the In-ter-pre-ter, who with the oil of His grace feeds the work in the heart; so that in spite of all the Dev-il can do, the souls of His saints still keep that grace. And as the man stood back of the wall to feed the fire, this is to teach you that it is hard for those who are tried to see how this work of grace is fed in the soul.

Then the In-ter-pre-ter led Chris-tian to a place where there was a King's House, fair to see. This sight made Chris-tian glad. He saw, too, some who stood on the top of it in robes of gold. Then said Chris-tian, May we go in?

The In-ter-pre-ter led him up to the door, where stood a host of men whose wish it was to go in, but they did not dare to. Near the door there sat a man at a desk, with a book and ink, to take the names of those who should go in. He saw, too, that in the door stood men clad in cast plates, to keep it, who sought to do all the hurt they could to those who went in. Chris-tian knew not what to make of this. At last, when all men shrank back for fear of the men at arms, Chris-tian saw a brave man* come up to the one who sat there to write and say, Set down my name, Sir, and when this was done he saw the man draw his sword, put a cast head piece on his head, and rush on the men at arms in the door, who struck at him with all their might. But the man did not at all lose heart, but cut and thrust with fierce blows. So when he had made and got not a few wounds, he at last cut his way through the midst of all who tried to keep him out, and made his way in, at which a sweet voice was heard from those who stood on the house top which sang: *Come in! Come in! Joy for all time you shall win!*

So he went in, and was clad with such robes as they. Then Chris-tian said, with a smile, I think I know what this means! But when he would have gone on, the In-ter-pre-ter said, No, stay till I have shown you more.

Then the In-ter-pre-ter led Chris-tian by the hand to a dark room, where sat a man in an I-ron Cage. Now the man, as I did look on him, did seem quite sad. He sat with his eyes cast down to the ground, his hands in tight clasp, and his sighs were such as would break the heart. When Chris-tian was told to talk with the man he said to him, What are you?

MAN. I am not what I was once.

CHRIS-TIAN. What were you once?

MAN. I was once a saint, in my own eyes, and in the eyes of all who saw me. I was, as I thought, sure to reach Mount Zi-on, and had much joy in this thought.

CHRIS-TIAN. Well, what are you now?

MAN. I am a man from whom hope has fled, and I am so shut up in this I-ron Cage that I can not get out; Oh, no, I can not!

CHRIS-TIAN. How did you come to be in this state?

MAN. I did not watch and pray; I laid the reins on the neck of my lusts; I went on in sin in spite of the light of the Word and the grace of God. I have brought grief to the Ho-ly Spir-it, and

---

* This brave man is called by Bunyan, a man of very stout countenance. He represents those whom Jesus spoke of who strive to enter by the narrow door, while those on the outside of the King's house, who did not dare try to go in, are those who seek to enter but are not able.

He is gone; the Dev-il has come to me. God, in His wrath, has left me, and I have made my heart so hard that I can not turn back to do what is right.

Then Chris-tian said to the In-ter-pre-ter, Is there no hope for such a man as this? He told him to ask him. So Chris-tian said, Is there no hope, but that you must be kept in this Cage?

MAN. No; none of all.

CHRIS-TIAN. Why? The Son of God is full of grace.

MAN. I have put Him once more to the Cross. My scorn has been on Him and His grace and His blood. I have shut my self out from all His words of good hope, and threats are all that are left for me—sure threats of wrath to come.

CHRIS-TIAN. For what did you bring this fate on your self?

MAN. For the lusts, joys, and gains of this world, in which I thought I could find great good, but now each one of them bites me like a worm of fire.

CHRIS-TIAN. But can you not now turn from your sin?

MAN. No, God hath shut me up in this I-ron Cage; nor can all the men in the world let me out, and the time to turn from my sins is past. Oh, what of the life that shall not end! How shall I bear with the wrath and pain I shall meet with in the next life that shall not end?

Then said In-ter-pre-ter to Chris-tian, Keep this man's woe in mind for your own good. This is a dread sight, said Chris-tian. God help me to watch and pray, that I may shun the cause of this man's woe. But is it not time for me to go on my way, Sir?

IN-TER-PRE-TER. Wait till I show you one thing more, and then you shall go.

Then In-ter-pre-ter took Chris-tian by the hand and led him to a room where was a man who, as he rose from his bed and put on his clothes, shook with fear. Why does this man shake thus? said Chris-tian. The In-ter-pre-ter told him to tell Chris-tian the cause, so he said, This night, when I slept, I had a dream, and the skies grew black, and did so roar and flash with fire that I was full of fear. Then I saw the clouds rack in a strange way and heard a great sound of a trump, and saw a Man who sat on a cloud, and with him were the hosts of Hea-ven. These all were in a flame of fire, and the skies were in a flame as well. Then I heard a voice say, rise, ye dead, and come

flame as well. Then I heard a voice say, rise, ye dead, and come to meet the Judge. And with that the rocks rent, the graves gave up their dead. Some of them were most glad and looked up to Hea-ven, and some cried to the rocks to hide them.

Then I saw a Man that sat on the cloud take the book and bid the world draw near. Yet, by means of a fierce flame that went to and fro in front of Him, a space was kept which they could not pass, as it is with the judge and the men at the bar in a court. Then I heard it said to the hosts who were with Him who sat on the cloud, Bind the tares and the chaff and cast them in the Lake of Fire. And with that I saw the earth on top of the pit of Hell split near where I stood, and out of the mouth of it came smoke and coals of fire, with shrieks of woe. Then it was said to the same hosts of Hea-ven, Bring my wheat to the store house, and I saw not a few caught up to the clouds, but I was left. I sought to hide, but could not for the Man that sat on the cloud still kept his eye on me. My sins all came to mind, and the voice of God in my soul showed me my guilt. Then I woke from my sleep.

CHRIS-TIAN. But what was there in this sight which made you fear so much?

MAN. I thought the day had come when I must meet the Judge, and I was not fit for it. But my great fright was that when some were caught up on high, I was left on the edge of the pit of hell. My sins, too, hurt me, and I thought the Judge kept his eye on me, and there was wrath in his gaze.

Then the In-ter-pre-ter told Chris-tian to keep these things in mind, so that they might be as a goad to prick him on in the Way he must go, and as Chris-tian set out once more on his Way, the In-ter-pre-ter said, The Lord be with you, good Chris-tian, to guide you in the Way that leads to Mount Zi-on.

Then I saw in my dream that the high way up which Chris-tian was to go had a wall on each side, and the name of that wall was Sal-va-tion. Up this high way did Chris-tian run, but with great toil 'cause of the load on his back. He ran thus till he drew near to a place on which stood a Cross, and at the foot of it a tomb. Just as Chris-tian came up to the Cross, his load fell from his back, and did roll till it came to the mouth of the tomb, where it fell in, and I saw it no more.

Then was Chris-tian glad, and said with a heart full of joy: He gives me rest by His grief, and life by His death. Yet he stood still for a while, for he was struck with awe to think that the sight of the cross should thus ease him of his load. Three or four times did he look on the cross and the tomb, and the tears rose to his eyes. As he stood thus and wept, lo, three Bright Ones came to him, and one of them said: Peace be to thee! Thy sins be made void, you are clean in front of God. And one came up to him to strip him of his rags and put new clothes on him, while the third set a mark on his fore head, and gave him a scroll with a seal on it, which he bid him look on as he ran, and give it in at the Gate of the Ce-les-ti-al Ci-ty; and then they left him.

Chris-tian gave three leaps for joy, and sang as he went: Ah, what a place is this! Here did the strings crack that bound my load to me. Blest cross! Blest tomb! Nay, blest is the Lord that was put to shame there for me!

I saw then in my dream that he went on thus, even till he came to a hill, where he saw, a few steps out of the way, three men who were in a sound sleep, with chains on their feet. The name of one was Sim-ple*, one Sloth*, and the third Pre-sump-tion*. As Chris-tian saw them lie in this state, he went to wake them, and said: You are like those that sleep on the top of a mast, for the Dead Sea is at your feet. Wake, rise, and come

---

* Simple might best be likened to the Biblical fool so aptly described by Solomon in Proverbs and Ecclesiastes: Fools despise wisdom and instruction (Proverbs 1:7); for folly is joy to him who lacks sense (Proverbs 15:21). His foolish heart has directed him to the wrong way (Ecclesiastes 10:2), but he is unaware of any danger in the path he has chosen. As a youth, he may have rejected the discipline of his father (Proverbs 15:5) and has reaped the fruit of his folly. He cannot even walk along the road, but all see his foolishness (Ecclesiastes 10:3). He multiplies words, but all his talk is folly and madness (Ecclesiastes 10:13). As a dog returns to his own vomit, so the fool returns to his own folly (Proverbs 26:11). His response to Christian is classic for the fool: 'I see no danger.'

* Sloth is lazy and is content to sleep a little out of the Way, yet he is wiser in his own conceit than seven men who can render a reason. He would be content to gain religion if it would drop into his mouth like a ripe fig, while he is laying on his bed. "He is content with a life of utter uselessness. He wilfully gives himself up to it; as if indolence was his supreme good...Every hour's indulgence strengthens the habit, and chains the victim in hopeless bondage" (Proverbs, Charles Bridges, pp. 460, 461).

* Presumption is so convinced of his good condition that he scorns the counsel of Christian and insists that he is ready to face God and believes he will fare well when he does. "Self-confidence fears no danger. 'I can look to myself; I need not go too far, and I shall get no harm.'" (Proverbs, Charles Bridges, p. 65).

CHRISTIAN IN VIEW OF THE CROSS.

with me. Trust me, and I will help you off with your chains. He, too, told them, If he that goes 'round like a fierce Li-on comes by, you will be a prey for his teeth. With that they cast their eyes up to look at him, and Sim-ple said, I see no cause for fear, and Sloth spoke, Yet a bit more sleep for me. Pre-sumption said, Let each man look to his own. And so they lay down to sleep once more, and Chris-tian went on his way, yet sad that the men had not left their sleep.

Then I saw in my dream that two men did climb the wall and jumped on to the left side of The Nar-row Way and made great haste to come up to him. Their names were For-mal-ist* and Hy-poc-ri-sy*.

CHRIS-TIAN. Sirs, whence come you, and where do you go?

FOR-MAL-IST and HY-POC-RI-SY. We were born in the land of Vain-Glo-ry, and are on our way to Mount Zi-on for praise.

CHRIS-TIAN. Why came you not in at the Gate? Know you not that he that comes not in at the door, but climbs the wall to get in, the same is a thief.

They told him that to go through the Gate was too far 'round, and that the best way was to make a short cut of it, and climb the wall as they had done.

CHRIS-TIAN. But will it not be a sin in the eyes of the Lord of the town where we are bound, if we do not go in the Way of His will?

They told Chris-tian that he had no need for care on that score, for long use had made it just like a law, and they could prove that it had been so for years.

CHRIS-TIAN. But are you quite sure that your way will stand up in a court of law?

Yes, said they, no doubt of it. Long use will be a sure plea with a fair judge. And if we get in The Nar-row Road, who cares which way we get in? If we are in, we are in; you are in the Way, who came in at the Gate, and we too are in the Way that choose to climb the wall. Is not our case as good as yours?

---

* Formalist is one whose religion consists of rituals, ceremonies, and creeds, but who does not know God in his heart, nor worship Him in truth. He worships a "god" to his own liking that he has created in his own imagination.

* Hypocrisy serves God for his own personal gain, so that he might be praised by men, get more business for his trade, or some similar reason. He may deliberately try to fool men, or he may be deceived himself, not even realizing that his pretended service to God is vain.

FORMALIST & HYPOCRISY COMING INTO THE WAY OVER THE WALL

CHRIS-TIAN. I walk by the rule of my Lord, but you walk by the rule of your own lusts. The Lord of the Way will count you as thieves, and you will not be found true men at the end of the Way. You come in with no aid from Him, and shall go out with no grace from Him.

To this, they just bade him look to him self. The three went on, each in his own way, with not much talk, save that the two men told Chris-tian that they did not doubt that they should keep all laws as well as he. We do not see, said they, where we are not like you, save in that cloak on your back, which, we doubt not, some friend gave you to hide your shame.

CHRIS-TIAN. Laws will not save those who come not in by the door; and as for this cloak on my back, the Lord of the place

29

which I seek gave it to me, as you say, to hide my shame; for I had nought but rags. And so, as I go on, I cheer my heart with the thought that when I come to the Gate of the Ce-les-ti-al Ci-ty the Lord will know me by His cloak, which I have on my back. It was His free gift in the day when He took my rags from me. I have, too, a mark on my fore head, which you may not have seen, which one of my Lord's friends put there the day that my load fell from my back. He gave me, too, a scroll with his seal, to cheer me as I go on the Way, and this I was told to give in at the Gate, to make sure that I can go in. You have none of these things, for you did not come in at the Gate. This made the men laugh, but they said not a word.

Then they all went on, but Chris-tian kept in front, and had no more talk but with his own heart, and was glad and sad by turns. He read much in his scroll, and this gave him strength.

I saw then that they all went on till they came to the foot of the Hill Dif-fi-cul-ty, where there was a spring. There were in the same place two more ways, one on the left hand and one on the right; but the Nar-row Way that Chris-tian was told to take went straight up the hill, and the name of the hill is Dif-fi-cul-ty, and he saw that the Way of life lay there.

Now when Chris-tian got as far as the Spring of Life he drank of it, and then went up the hill saying, Best the Right Way to go, Than wrong, where the end is woe. But when the two men saw that it was steep and high, and that there were three ways to choose from, one of them took the path the name of which is Dan-ger, and lost his way in a great wood, and one of them went by the road of De-struc-tion, which led him to a wide field full of dark rocks, where he fell, and rose no more. I then saw Chris-tian go up the hill, where at first I could see him run, then walk, and then go on his hands and knees, 'cause the hill was so steep.

Now half way up was an Ar-bour made by the Lord of the Hill, so that those who came by might rest there. Here Chris-tian sat down, and took out the scroll and read it, till at last he fell off in a deep sleep which kept him there till it was dusk; and while he slept his scroll fell from his hand. At length a man came up to him and woke him, and said: Go to the ant, thou man of sloth, and learn of her to be wise. At this Chris-tian gave a start, and sped on his way, and went at a quick pace.

CHRISTIAN MEETS MISTRUST AND TIMOROUS.

E. WENTWORTH Sc.

When he had got near to the top of the hill, two men came up to him who did run back from the way that led to Mount Zi-on, whose names were Tim-or-ous and Mis-trust*, to whom Chris-tian said, Sirs, what ails you? You run the wrong way.

Tim-or-ous said that they were on the way to Mount Zi-on, but that when they had got half way they found they met with more and more risk, so that great fear came on them, and all they could do was to turn back.

Yes, said Mis-trust, for just in front of us there lay two Li-ons in the Way; we knew not if they slept or not, but we thought that they would fall on us and tear our limbs off.

CHRIS-TIAN. You fill me with fear. Where shall I fly to be safe? If I go back to my own town of De-struc-tion, I am sure to lose my life, for it shall be burned with fire from Hea-ven, but if I can get to The Ce-les-tial Ci-ty, there I shall be safe. To turn back is death; to go on is fear of death, but when I come there, a life of bliss that knows no end. I will yet go on.

So Mis-trust and Tim-or-ous ran down the hill and Chris-tian went on his way. Yet he thought once more of what he had heard from the men, and then he felt in his cloak for his scroll, that he might read it and find some peace, but when He felt for it, he found it not.

Then was Chris-tian in great grief, and knew not what to do for the lack of that which was to be his pass in to the Ce-les-ti-al Ci-ty. At last, thought he: I slept in the Ar-bour by the side of the hill. So he fell down on his knees to pray that God would cleanse his sin for this act; and then went back to look for his scroll. But as he went, what tongue can tell the grief of Chris-tian's heart? Oh, vile man that I am! said he, to sleep in the day time. Some times he did sigh, some times he wept, and he did chide him self that he was such a fool to sleep in that place which was built by the Lord of the hill just to make fresh the tired and soothe the soul.

So he went back, and with much care did he look on this side

---

* Timorous and Mistrust are afraid of unknown risks and dangers even though they have no certain knowledge of what the dangers are, nor have they given any thought as to how they might be overcome. They are as the slothful man in Proverbs 26:13: "The slothful man saith, There is a lion in the way; a lion is in the streets." They walk by sight and feelings and not by faith.

CHRISTIAN DISCOVERS HIS LOST ROLL IN THE ARBOUR

and on that for his scroll. At length he came near to the Ar-bour where he had sat and slept. How far, thought Chris-tian, have I gone in vain! Such was the lot of the Jews for their sin; they were sent back by the way of the Red Sea; and I am made to tread those steps with grief which I might have trod with joy, had it not been for this sleep. How far might I have been on my Way by this time! I am made to tread those steps thrice which I need not to have trod but once; yea, now too I am like to be lost in the night, for the day is well nigh spent. O that I had not slept!

Now by this time he had come to the Ar-bour once more, where for a while he sat down and wept; but at last as he cast a sad glance at the foot of the bench, he saw his scroll, which he caught up with haste, and put in his cloak. Who can tell the great joy Chris-tian felt when he had found his scroll? He gave thanks to God and with what a light step did he now climb the hill!

But, ere he got to the top, the sun went down on Chris-tian, and this made him call to mind how he had slept in the day time. O that sin-filled sleep! Then he did think of Tim-or-ous and Mis-trust and how they had told him of their fear of the Li-ons in the Way. Ah, thought he, these beasts range in the night for their prey; and if they should meet with me in the dark, how should I fly from them?

Still Chris-tian went on, and while he thought thus on his sad lot, he cast up his eyes and saw a great house in front of him, the name of which was Beau-ti-ful, and it stood just by the side of the high road. So he made haste and went on in the hope that he could rest there a while. And soon he saw that two Li-ons stood in his way. Then he thought, I see now the cause of all those fears that drove Mis-trust and Tim-or-ous back (the Li-ons were bound with chains, but he saw not the chains). Then fear seized him for he saw death in front of him. The name of the man who kept the lodge of that house was Watch-ful, and when he saw that Chris-tian made a halt as if he would go back, he came out to him and said: Is your strength so small? Fear not the two Li-ons, for they are bound by chains, and are put here to try the faith of those that have it, and to find out those that have none. Keep in the midst of the path and no harm shall come to you.

Then I saw that still he went on in great dread of the Li-ons, but did as Watch-ful told him, and though he heard them roar, yet they did him no harm; but when he had gone by them he clapt his hands and went on till he came and stood in front of the Gate where Watch-ful was.

CHRIS-TIAN. Sir, what house is this? May I rest here this night?

WATCH-FUL. This house was built by the Lord of the Hill to give aid to Pil-grims. Tell me, Where do you come from?

CHRIS-TIAN. I am come from the Ci-ty of De-struc-tion, and am on my way to Mount Zi-on; but the day is far spent, and I would, if I may, spend the night here.

WATCH-FUL. What is your name?

34

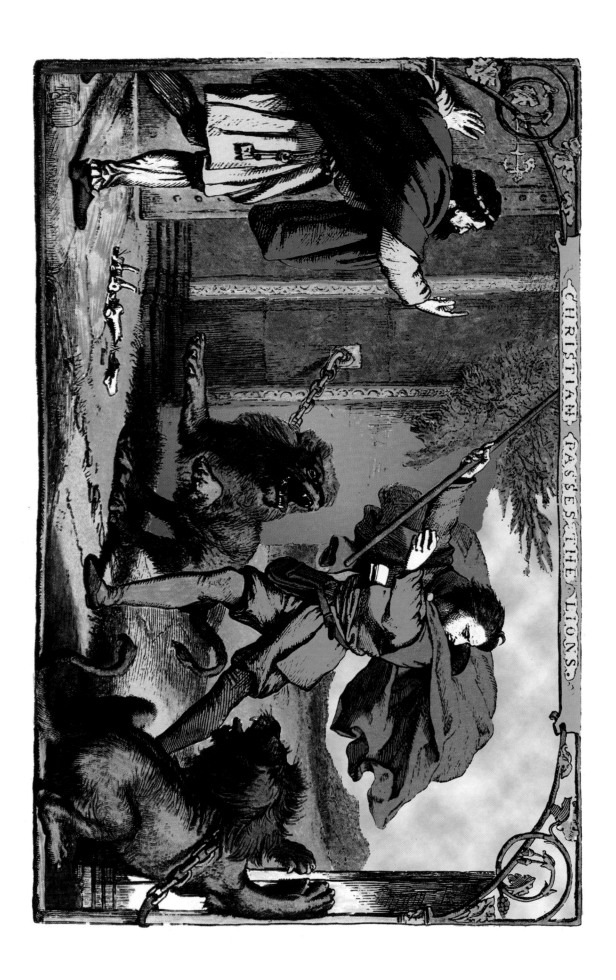

CHRISTIAN PASSES THE LIONS.

CHRIS-TIAN. My name is now Chris-tian, but at first it was Grace-less.

WATCH-FUL. How is it you came so late? The sun is set.

Chris-tian then told him how he had slept, and lost his roll.

WATCH-FUL. Well, I will call one that lives here, who, if she likes your talk, will let you come in, for these are the rules of the house. So he rang a bell, at the sound of which there came out at the door a grave and fair maid, whose name was Dis-cre-tion*. When Watch-ful told her why Chris-tian had come there, she said to him: What is your name?

It is Chris-tian, he said, and I much wish to rest here to-night, and the more so for I see this place was built by the Lord of the Hill, to shield those from harm who come to it.

So she gave a smile, but the tears stood in her eyes; and in a short time she said: I will call forth two or three more of our house; and then she ran to the door and brought in Pru-dence*, Pi-e-ty*, and Char-i-ty*, who did more talk with him and then said: Come in, thou blest of the Lord: this house was built by the Lord of the Hill for such as you. Then Chris-tian did bow down his head, and went with them to the house.

PI-E-TY. Come, good Chris-tian, since our love prompts us to take you in to rest, let us talk with you of all that you have seen on your Way.

CHRIS-TIAN. With a right good will, and I am glad that you should ask it of me. Then Chris-tian told them why he left the Ci-ty of De-struc-tion, of his stay at the house of the In-ter-pre-ter, how his great load fell off at the Cross, and of all else that he saw and did on the Way.

PRU-DENCE. And, first, tell us what is it that makes you wish so much to go to Mount Zi-on?

CHRIS-TIAN. Why there I hope to see Him that did die on the Cross; and there I hope to be rid of all those things that to this day grieve and vex me. There, they say, is not death; and there I shall dwell with such as love the Lord.

CHAR-I-TY. Have you a wife and young ones?

---

* Discretion - Discernment; individual judgment.

* Prudence - The ability to regulate and discipline oneself through the exercise of reason.

* Piety - Dutifulness in religion; devoutness.

* Charity - Christian love; the act or feeling of affection or benevolence.

Christian enters the Palace.

CHRIS-TIAN. Yes, I have a wife and four small boys.

CHAR-I-TY. And why did you not bring them with you?

Then Chris-tian wept, and said: On, how glad should I have been to do so! But they would not come with me, nor have me leave them, nor did they want me to head to Mount Zi-on.

CHAR-I-TY. But what did they say as to why they would not come?

CHRIS-TIAN. Why, my wife was scared to lose this world; and my young ones did take their joy in the things of fools.

CHAR-I-TY. You should have spake to them to try to show them the fear of what would come on them if they did not join you.

CHRIS-TIAN. So I did; and told them what God did show me of what was to come to the Ci-ty of De-struc-tion; but they did mock me and did not trust what I said.

CHAR-I-TY. And did you pray to God to put it in their hearts to go with you?

CHRIS-TIAN. Yes, and that with much warmth, for you may think how dear they were to me.

Now I saw in my dream that they did thus talk till it came time to eat. Then they sat down to meat and all of their talk then was of the Lord of the Hill; as, what He had done, why He did what He did, why He had built that House, and how He had slain him that had the strength of Death on his side, which made me love Him more. Thus did Chris-tian talk with these friends till it grew dark, and then he took his rest in a large room, the name of which was Peace; there he slept till break of day, and then he sang a hymn.

They told him that he should not leave till they had shown him all the rare things that were in that place. There were to be seen the rod of Mo-ses, the nail with which Ja-el slew Sis-er-a, the lamps with which Gid-e-on put to flight the host of Mid-i-an, and the ox goad with which Sham-gar slew his foes. And they brought out the jaw bone of an ass with which Sam-son did such great feats, and the sling and stone with which Da-vid slew Go-li-ath of Gath, and some more things, which Chris-tian saw with joy. This done, they went to their rest.

Then I saw in my dream that Chris-tian rose to take his leave of Dis-cre-tion, and of Pru-dence, Pi-e-ty, and Char-i-ty, but they said that he must stay till the next day, that they might show him the De-lec-ta-ble Moun-tains, so they took him to the top of the house, and told him look to the south, which he did, and lo, a great way off, he saw a rich land, full of hills, woods, vines, fruits of all kinds, and streams.

What is the name of this land? said Chris-tian.

Then they told him it was Im-man-u-el's Land. And, they said, It is as much meant for you, and the like of you, as this hill is; and when you reach the place, there you may see the Gate of The Ce-les-tial Ci-ty.

Then they took him to the Ar-mor-y and clothed him from head to foot with cast plates and gave him a sword, lest he should meet some foe in the way; and they went with him

CHRISTIAN armed by PRUDENCE, DISCRETION, PIETY & CHARITY.

down the hill. Watch-ful told him that a man had just gone by who said his name was Faith-ful.

Oh! said Chris-tian, I know him; his home was near mine; he comes from the place where I was born. How far do you think he has gone?

WATCH-FUL. He is by this time at the foot of the hill.

CHRIS-TIAN. Then said Chris-tian, The Lord be with you, kind Watch-ful, and may He do good to you for what you have done for me. Oh, of a truth, said Chris-tian, it is as great a toil to come down the hill as it was to go up.

PRU-DENCE. So it is, for it is a hard thing for a man to go down to The Val-ley of Hu-mil-i-a-tion, as you do now, and for this cause have we come with you to the foot of the hill. So, though he went with great care, yet he caught a slip or two.

Then in my dream I saw that when they had got to the foot of the hill, these good friends of Chris-tian's gave him a loaf of bread, a flask of wine, and some sun dried grapes; and then they left him to go on his Way.

But now in this Val-ley of Hu-mil-i-a-tion poor Chris-tian was hard put to it, for he had not gone far, ere he saw a foul fiend come through the field to meet him, whose name was A-pol-lyon*. Then did Chris-tian fear, and he cast in his mind if he would go back or stand his ground. But Chris-tian thought that as he had no cast plates on his back, to turn 'round might give A-pol-lyon a chance to pierce it with his darts. So he stood his ground, for, thought he, if but to save my life were all I had in view, still the best way would be to stand.

Now the fiend was foul to look on; he had scales like a fish (and these are his pride); he had great wings, and feet like a bear, and out of him came fire and smoke, and his mouth was as the mouth of the king of beasts. So he went on, and A-pol-lyon met him with looks of scorn.

A-POL-LYON. Where do you come from and to what place are you bound?

---

* Apollyon's name means the destroyer. He is depicted in the Scriptures by many names including the angel of the bottomless pit (Revelation 9:11), the great dragon, old serpent, the Devil, Satan (Revelation 12:9), and called by Christ a murderer, a liar, and the father of lies (John 8:44). Here is Christian's battle with the powers of hell and the depiction of the fierce assaults of the Devil (I Peter 5:8 & Ephesians 6:11-13), determined either to turn him back to his old life or destroy him so that he can do no good to others.

CHRISTIAN'S COMBAT WITH APOLLYON

CHRIS-TIAN. I am come from The Ci-ty of De-struc-tion, which is the place of all sin, and I am on my way to the Ci-ty of Zi-on.

A-POL-LYON. By this I see you are mine, for all that land is mine, I am the Prince and God of it. How is it, then, that you have left your king? Were it not that I have a hope that you may do me more good, I would strike you to the ground with one blow.

CHRIS-TIAN. I was born in your realm, it is true, but you drove us too hard, and your pay was such as no man could live on, for the pay for sin is death

A-POL-LYON. No prince likes to lose his men, nor will I as yet lose you; so if you will come back, what my realm yields I will give you.

CHRIS-TIAN. But I am bound by vows to the King of Kings, and how can I be true to Him and go back with you?

A-POL-LYON. You have made a change, it seems, from bad to worse; but some times those who say they are His give Him the slip, and come back to me.

CHRIS-TIAN. I gave Him my faith, and swore to be true to Him: How can I go back from this?

A-POL-LYON. You did the same to me, and yet I will pass by all, if you will but turn and go back.

CHRIS-TIAN. When I swore faith to you I was not of age, and what is more, the Prince whose flag is now my boast, can clear me of that oath, and of all which I did to please you. And to speak truth, O thou Prince of Death, I like His work, His pay, His rule, His friends, and His land the best: so urge me no more. I am His, and shall go with Him.

A-POL-LYON. But think, while you are in cool blood, what you must meet with in this way of your choice. Most of those who serve Him come to an ill end for the wrong which they do me and my ways. What hosts of them have met a death of shame! How can you count it best to serve Him when He has not once come from the place where He is to save those who serve Him from their foes; while, as all the world knows, time and time I have saved, by might or fraud, those who have served me, from Him and His, and so will I save you.

CHRIS-TIAN. He does not come at once to save them, that He may try their love, and see if they will cleave to Him to the end, and as for the ill end to which you have said they come, that is most to their praise. They do not look for much ease now, but wait for their crown, and they shall have it when their Prince comes in all his pomp, with the An-gels of God.

A-POL-LYON. You have been false to Him so soon, and how do you think He will give you a crown?

CHRIS-TIAN. Where have I been false to Him, O A-pol-lyon?

A-POL-LYON. You did faint in the first start, when you were in the Slough of De-spond. You did try wrong ways to be rid of your load, and did not wait till your Prince should take it off. You did sleep, and lost your choice things. The sight of the Li-ons made you long to go back; and in all your talk of what you have seen and heard on the Way, you are, at heart, vain and seek praise.

CHRIS-TIAN. All this is true, and much more which you have left out; but the Prince whom I serve is full of grace, and He can cleanse my sins. But these weak traits were mine when I was yet in your land; there I got them, and they made me groan and mourn till I sought and found peace with my Prince.

Then A-pol-lyon broke out in great rage, and said: I am a foe to this Prince; I hate Him, His laws, His friends. I have come out to fight you.

Then said Chris-tian, A-pol-lyon, take care what you do, for I am on the King's high way; so take heed to your self.

A-POL-LYON. I am void of fear. You shall no more go this Way. Here on this spot I will put you to death. With that he threw a dart of fire at his breast, but Chris-tian had a shield on his arm, with which he caught it. Then did Chris-tian draw his sword, for he saw it was time to stir; and A-pol-lyon as fast made at him, and threw darts as thick as hail; with which in spite of all that Chris-tian could do, A-pol-lyon gave him wounds in his head, hand, and foot.

This made Chris-tian draw back a bit, but A-pol-lyon still came on, and Chris-tian once more took heart. They fought for half a day, till Chris-tian, weak from his wounds, was well nigh spent in strength. When A-pol-lyon saw this, he threw him down with great force; and with that Chris-tian's sword fell out of his hand. Then said A-pol-lyon, I am sure of you now.

But while he strove to make an end of Chris-tian, that good man put out his hand in haste to feel for his sword, and caught it. Boast not, oh A-pol-lyon! he said, and with that he struck a blow which made his foe reel back as one that had had his last wound. Then A-pol-lyon spread out his wings and fled, so that Chris-tian saw him no more.

When the fight was at an end Chris-tian gave thanks to Him who did help and save him from A-pol-lyon. Then there came to him a hand which held some leaves of the Tree of Life; some of them Chris-tian took, and as soon as he had put them to his wounds, he saw them heal up at once. He sat down in that place to eat bread and drank from the flask which the maids gave him, and then set out once more on his Way, with his sword drawn in his hand, lest more foes might be near. But A-pol-lyon met him no more in this vale.

Now near this place was the Val-ley of the Shad-ow of Death, and Chris-tian must needs go through it to get to the Ce-les-ti-al Ci-ty. It was a land of drought and full of pits, a land that no man (but a Chris-tian) could pass through, and where no man dwelt. So that here he was worse put to it than in his fight with A-pol-lyon, which by and by we shall see.

As he drew near the Shad-ow of Death he met with two men, sons of them that brought a bad tale of the good land, who ran with their backs to the Ce-les-ti-al Ci-ty, to whom Chris-tian thus spoke: To what place do you go?

MEN. Back! Back! And we would have you do the same if you prize life and peace.

CHRIS-TIAN. But why?

MEN. We went on as far as we did dare go.

CHRIS-TIAN. What have you seen?

MEN. Seen! Why the Val-ley of the Shad-ow of Death which is dark as pitch; but by good luck we caught sight of what lay in front of us, ere we came up. We saw there ghosts and imps and fiends of the pit; we heard the howls and yells of men in great pain, who sat there bound in woe and chains; and Death does spread his wings there day and night.

CHRIS-TIAN. I see not yet, by what you have told me, but that this is the Way to Zi-on.

MEN. Be it your Way then; we will not choose it for ours.

So they took their leave, and Chris-tian went on, but still with his drawn sword in his hand, for fear lest he should meet once more with a foe.

I saw then in my dream that so far as this Val-ley went, there was on the right hand a deep ditch; that ditch to which the blind have led the blind as long as the world has been made.

And lo, on the left hand there was a quag, in which if a man fall, he would find no firm ground for his foot to stand on.

Here the path of Chris-tian was a mere line, and so good Chris-tian was the more put to it; for when he sought in the dark to shun the ditch on the one hand, he was close to the quag, and when he sought to flee from the quag, he had to use great care lest he should fall in the ditch.

Thus he went on, and I heard him sigh; for still more to vex him, the path was here so dark that when he would lift his foot to go on, he knew not where or on what he should set it next.

CHRISTIAN IN THE VALLEY of the SHADOW of DEATH.

Near the midst of the Val-ley was the mouth of Hell as I saw, and it stood close to the way side. Now what shall I do, thought Chris-tian, and such a mass of flame and smoke came out with sparks, and with such dread sounds—things that did not care for Chris-tian's sword, as A-pol-lyon had done—that he had to put up his sword and take up new arms, All-Prayer by name. So I heard him cry, O Lord, save my soul!

Thus he went on a great while, and the flames leapt at him, and he heard sad wails, and a rush of feet, which ran to and fro, so that he thought they would tear him in shreds, or tread him down, like the mire in the streets. For miles and miles he saw and heard these dread things, and, at last, when he thought he heard a band of fiends, who were on their way to meet him, he stood still to think what he had best do.

At times he had half a thought he would go back; but then he thought that he might be half way through the Val-ley. He thought, too, of all that he had gone through, and that it might be worse to go back than to go on. So he made up his mind to go on, but the fiends did seem to draw quite near. But when they had come at him, as it were, he cried out with all his might: I will walk in the strength of the Lord God. So they gave back.

One thing I must not let slip. I saw that now poor Chris-tian was in such a state that he did not know his own voice; and this is how I found it out. Just when he had come to the mouth of the pit, one of the imps crept up by stealth to hiss vile things in his ear, which Chris-tian thought came from his own mind. This was worst of all to Chris-tian—that he should have such base thoughts of Him for whom his love had been so great. He did not wish to do it; but he had not the wit to stop his ears, or to know from whence these vile words came.

At last he thought he heard the voice of a man in front of him, who said, Though I walk through the Val-ley of the Shad-ow of Death, I will fear no ill, for Thou art with me.

Then was he glad, for he was sure that some of God's saints must be in this place as well as he, and that God was with them. And why not with me, too? he said, though I can not see them in this dark place, and he had the hope that he might catch up to them and be with them soon.

So he went on, and cried to him whose voice he had heard, but the man did not speak to Chris-tian for he too thought

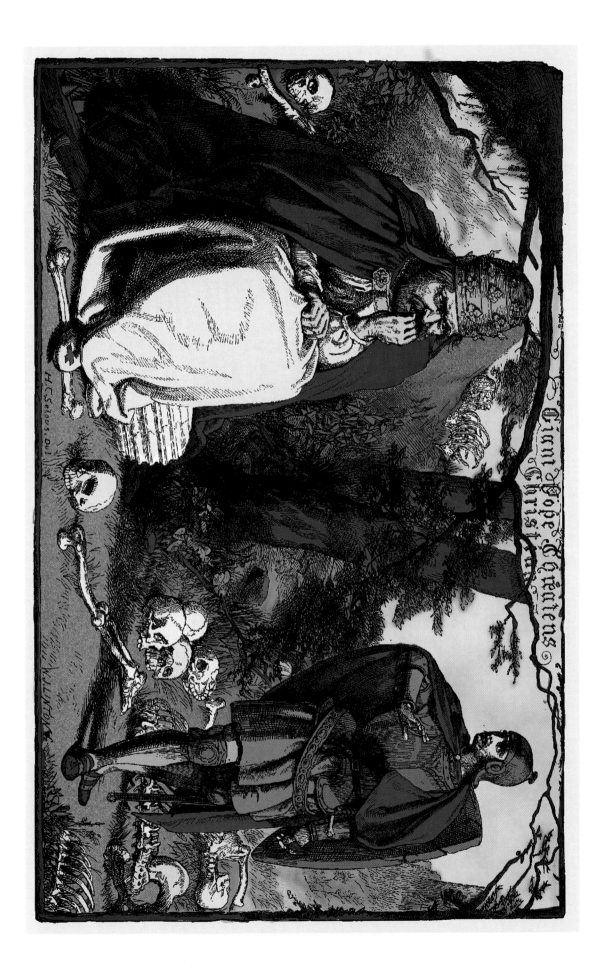

Giant Pope Pagan
Christian

that he was a lone Pil-grim. By and by day broke, and Chris-tian said, He doth turn the night of death to day light.

By the light of day he could see more of the risks he had run; the ditch on his side and the quag on that, and what a mere thread the path was. He saw, too, the ghosts, and imps, and fiends of the pit, but all were far off, for when day broke they did not come near him.

The sun now rose, and this was a great help to Chris-tian, for the rest of the way was worse than the first, if that could be. All the way to the end was set so full of snares, traps, gins and nets here, and pits and deep holes there, that if it had now been dark as at first and had he had scores of souls, they might all have been lost; but as I said just now, the sun rose.

Then Chris-tian said: His sun shines on my head, and by His light I go through the dark. In this light he came to the end of the Val-ley.

Now I saw in my dream that at the end of the Val-ley there lay blood and bones, the dust and torn flesh of men who had gone this way in past times. While I thought what the cause might be, I spied near me a cave where Gi-ant Pope and Gi-ant Pa-gan dwelt in old times, by whom these men whose blood, bones, and dust lay near by, had been put to death. But Chris-tian went by with not much harm. I knew not why till I heard that Pa-gan has been dead this long time, and Pope, though he still lives, yet through great age, and the hard rubs he got in his youth, has so lost his wits and is so stiff in the joints, that all he can do is to sit in his cave's mouth and grin at those who pass by, and bite his nails in rage that he can not get at them.

So I saw that Chris-tian went on, yet at the sight of the old man at the mouth of the cave he knew not what to think, and all the more when, though he could not reach him, yet the old man cried, You will not mend till we burn more of you! But Chris-tian held his peace and set a good face on it, and so went by and caught no hurt.

Now as Chris-tian went on, he found there was a rise in the road, which had been thrown up that Pil-grims might see what lay in front of them. Up this road Chris-tian went, and saw Faith-ful a short way off. Then said Christ-tian: Ho! Ho! Stay, and I will join you; but Faith-ful said, No; I flee for my life, and the sword of wrath is back of me.

At this Chris-tian put to all his strength, and soon got up with Faith-ful and ran by him; so the last was first. Then Chris-tian's face wore a vain smile at the thought that he had got the start of his friend; but as he did not take heed to his steps, all at once his foot caught and he fell, and could not rise till Faith-ful came to help him.

Then I saw that they went on side by side, in love, and had sweet talk of all they had met on the Way.

Thus did Chris-tian start, How long did you stay in the Ci-ty of De-struc-tion when you knew I had set out?

FAITH-FUL. Till I could stay no more, for there was great talk when you had gone that our town would soon burn to the ground with fire from Hea-ven.

CHRIS-TIAN. Why, then, did no one come with you?

FAITH-FUL. Though there was much talk of it, yet I doubt if they had true faith that these things would be so, for I heard them make sport of you and your course; but I was sure that the end of our town would be with fire from Hea-ven, and so I fled.

CHRIS-TIAN. What did they say of Pli-a-ble?

FAITH-FUL. I heard that he went with you till he came to the Slough of De-spond, where some say he fell in. He did not like to have it known; but I am sure he had much of that kind of dirt on him.

CHRIS-TIAN. What did they say to him?

FAITH-FUL. All sorts of men do mock and scorn him, and few will set him on work. He is far worse than if he had not left the town at all.

CHRIS-TIAN. But why should they do so, since they, too, scorn the Way which he has left?

FAITH-FUL. Oh, they say hang him! He is a turn coat! He was false to his vows.

CHRIS-TIAN. Did you talk with him?

FAITH-FUL. I met him once in the streets, but he made off, as if in shame at what he had done; so I did not speak to him.

CHRIS-TIAN. I had great hopes of that man when I first set out, but now I fear he will be lost when the town is burnt with fire. For it has come to pass with him as the true book says, The dog turns back to his puke once more; and the pig that was washed, to roll in the mire.

FAITH-FUL. These are my fears for him too, but who can stop that which will be?

CHRIS-TIAN. Well, my friend, let us leave him and talk of new things. Tell me, what did you meet with in the Way as you came?

FAITH-FUL. I did not fall in the Slough of De-spond as you did, but I did meet an old man at the foot of the Hill Dif-fi-cul-ty who did ask me What I was? and Where I did go? I told him that I was a Pil-grim on my way to the Ce-les-ti-al Ci-ty. Then the old man said to me, You look like a man of truth, will you dwell with me for the pay I will give you? I did ask his name and where he dwelt, and he said that his name was A-dam the First* and he lived in the town of De-ceit. I did ask him, What was his work? and What pay would he give? He told me that his work was heaps of joys and charms and that I would be his hier at the end; that his house was full to the brim of the fine things of the world and that he had three girls whose names were The Lust of the Flesh, The Lust of the Eyes, and The Pride of Life, and that I could wed them all, if I would. So I did ask him, How long a time he would have me to live with him? He said, As long as he lived him self.

CHRIS-TIAN. How did you and the old man end up?

FAITH-FUL. At first I thought I should go with the man, for he spoke quite well, but then I saw in his fore head the words, Put Off the Old Man with his Deeds, and it came hot to my mind that though he spoke well, when he got me to his house, he would sell me for a slave. So I told him I would not come near the door of his house.

CHRIS-TIAN. And what then?

FAITH-FUL. Then he did rant and rail at me, so I did turn from him to leave and just as I did so, I felt him take hold of my flesh, and he gave me a pinch so hard that I thought he had pulled a part of my flesh off. This made me cry, Oh, vile man! So I went my way.

---

* Adam the First represents the condition of men when they first come into the world. They are depraved and corrupt, slaves to sin and the lusts of the flesh. They live to please themselves and to gratify their own selfish desires. The indulge themselves in the lusts of the flesh, the lust of the eyes, and pursue the pride of life (the daughters of Adam the First). Unconverted men live as gods to themselves, and the world and all it offers is the means by which they achieve their end of self-worship.

FAITHFUL'S STRUGGLE WITH ADAM THE FIRST.

Then Chris-tian said, What else did you meet with on the Way? Faith-ful told him that he had met Wan-ton, Dis-content, and Shame, and they all had tried in vain to draw him from the right path. But he said that the sun had shone on him all through the Val-ley of Shad-ow of Death.

Then I saw in my dream, that as they went on, Faith-ful did look to one side and saw a man by the name of Talk-a-tive* who did walk a ways off from them. To this man Faith-ful said, Friend, where do you go? Are you on the way to the Ce-les-ti-al Ci-ty?

TALK-A-TIVE. I am on the way to that same place.

FAITH-FUL. That is well. I hope you may walk with us.

TALK-A-TIVE. With a good will, I will do so.

FAITH-FUL. Let us go on then and talk of things that are good.

TALK-A-TIVE. To talk of things that are good with you or some one else makes me glad. There are few that care to spend their time that way, but choose much to speak of things that do not aid one; and this hath hurt me.

FAITH-FUL. This is sad. The best use of the tongue of men on earth is to talk of God and Hea-ven.

TALK-A-TIVE. I like you much. What is so good as to think of the things of God? Why, if a man doth want to talk of things in the past, or the deep things of God, or signs, where shall he find them so well put down as in the Ho-ly Bi-ble? There a man may learn much, as the lack of real worth of the things of the world, the need of the new birth, that our works can not please God, the need of Christ, and more, as to turn from sin, to pray, and to put our trust in God.

FAITH-FUL. All this is true. I am glad to hear you say these things.

TALK-A-TIVE. The lack of this is the cause that so few know of true faith, the need of a work of grace in their souls, so that they may live on with out end. Men live as dumb fools and try

---

* Talkative is a man for whom the sum and substance of religion is to talk of the things of God. Christian sums him up superbly by saying, "Religion hath no place in his heart, or house, or conversation (life): all that he hath lieth in his tongue; and his religion is to make a noise therewith." Talkative speaks of the things of God, but his actions show that he is utterly devoid of the power of a changed heart and life. He holds to a form of godliness (so much so that good Faithful is, at first, deceived by his talk), but it is an outward form manifested merely by the flapping of his mouth (II Timothy 3:5).

to keep the works of the law, by which no man can get to Hea-ven.

FAITH-FUL. To know of the things of Hea-ven is the gift of God. No man can know them by works, or just to read of them, or by the talk of them by it self.

TALK-A-TIVE. All this I know quite well. All is of grace, not of works.

FAITH-FUL. What is the one thing at this time we shall talk on then?

TALK-A-TIVE. What you will. I will talk of things of Hea-ven or of the earth; things pure and right or things vile; things past or things to come, just so all is done to our good.

Now did Faith-ful start to think on what Talk-a-tive said, and did say to Chris-tian out of the ears of Talk-a-tive, For sure this man will make a great Pil-grim. At this Chris-tian smiled and said, This man, whom you like so well, will fool most who know him not. His name is Talk-a-tive and he dwells in our town. He is the son of one Say-Well. In spite of his tongue, he is a sad case.

FAITH-FUL. He seems to be a fine man.

CHRIS-TIAN. To those who do not know him he may seem so, for he is best when not at home. Near home his deeds are quite bad. He is for much talk. As he talks with you now, so he will talk on the ale bench as he gets drunk. God has no place in his heart, house, or life, though he speaks much of the things of God.

FAITH-FUL. Say you so! Then by this man I am fooled.

CHRIS-TIAN. Fooled! You may be sure of it. Call to mind the words of the good book: They say, and do not. He talks of the things of God, but it is all just talk. I have been in his house and I know what I say is true. His house is void of those things which please God. Those who know him say, He is a saint at large, and a Dev-il at home. He is a stain and shame to true Chris-tians. He has caused quite a few to fall by his life. Those who deal with him say that he lies and cheats them to gain wealth. All these things and a great deal more as bad, I know I can prove him to have guilt in.

FAITH-FUL. Well, now I see that to say and to do are not the same.

CHRIS-TIAN. They are two things for sure. This Talk-a-tive does not know. He thinks that to hear and to talk will make a man a good Chris-tian; thus he tricks his own soul. Let us be sure that at the day of doom, God will judge men by their fruit. It will not be said to them then, Did you have faith? But were you men who did the truth or just talk of it? And so they shall be judged.

Then Faith-ful stept up to where Talk-a-tive did walk and said, Come, how is it now?

TALK-A-TIVE. Thank you, well. I thought we should have had a great deal of talk by this time.

FAITH-FUL. If you will, we will fall to it now. Let us start with this: How does the Grace which saves prove it self, when it is in a man's heart?

TALK-A-TIVE. Why, to *know* of the deep things of the Gospel.

FAITH-FUL. A man may *know* much, and yet not be a child of God. When Christ said, Do you know all these things and the Dis-ci-ples said, Yes; Then He said, Blest are you if you *do* them. To know pleases those who like to talk and boast, but to do is that which doth please God. So this, your sign, is false.

TALK-A-TIVE. You lie in wait to trap me, this is not to build one up.

FAITH-FUL. Let me ask this: Are what you say and what you do the same? Does your faith in Christ show it self in word or tongue, and not in deed and truth? Say no more than God will say, Yes! to. For to say, I am thus and thus, when my life and friends tell me I lie, is a great sin.

Then Talk-a-tive did start to blush, and said, This type of talk I did not think we would have, nor will I make you my judge. Pray tell me, why do you ask such things?

FAITH-FUL. I saw you quick to talk, but to tell you the truth, I have heard of you, that you say you live for God, but your life shows that what you say is a lie. Chris-tians say you are a shame and spot to them; that some fall due to your bad life; that you lie, cheat, get drunk, and love to gain wealth.

TALK-A-TIVE. Since you are such a rash judge and not fit for fine talk, I will leave you.

Then Chris-tian came up and said, Your words and his lusts did not mix well with him. He would choose to leave than change his life. Let him go, the loss is no man's but his own. He would have been but a blot on us.

FAITH-FUL. I am glad we had this talk with him. He may think of it in the time to come. I have been plain with him, and so am clear of his blood, if he goes down to the pit.

CHRIS-TIAN. You did well to speak so plain to him. I wish that all men would deal such as you have done. The lack of such plain talk does make Chris-ti-an-i-ty stink to those in the world, who think all Chris-tians are like Talk-a-tive.

As they now had to pass through a no man's land, they would no doubt have found the way long had it not been that they could talk of what they had seen on the road. But when they were near the end of this plain, Faith-ful by chance cast a glance back, and saw E-van-gel-ist on their track.

It is my good friend, E-van-gel-ist, said Chris-tian. Yes, and my good friend, too, said Faith-ful, for it was he who set me on the way to the Gate. When he came up to them, he said, Peace be with you, dear friends, and peace be to those who help you.

Right glad am I to see you, my good E-van-gel-ist, said Chris-tian; the sight of your face brings to mind all your kind words and deeds for my good. And I am more than glad, said Faith-ful; how good it is, O sweet E-van-gel-ist, that we poor souls, can spend time with you.

Then said E-van-gel-ist, How has it fared with you, my friends, since we last met? What have you met with, and how have you stood your ground? So Chris-tian and Faith-ful told him all.

E-VAN-GEL-IST. Right glad am I, not that you have been so tried, but that you have won through it all, and are yet in the Way. I am glad for my own sake, and yours, for I have sown and you reap, and in due time you shall reap more if you faint not. The crown is held out to you, and it is one which will not fade. So run, that you may win it. Some set out to win it, and when they have gone far for it, some one comes and takes it from them; hold fast what you have, let no man take your crown. You are not yet out of the gun shot of the Dev-il. Let the sight of the Ce-les-ti-al Ci-ty be in your view and have faith in those things which are not seen. Look well to your own heart, and its lusts. Let your face be like a flint, and you will have all might in earth and the world to come on your side.

Then, with thanks for these words, they sought to learn more from E-van-gel-ist. Since he could see things to come, they would have him tell them what should fall to their lot on the Way, and how they could best meet it.

E-VAN-GEL-IST. My sons, you have read in God's Word that the way to Mount Zi-on lies through much pain and gloom. You have found this to be true so soon, and you will know more of it as you go on. You will soon come in sight of a town, and when you reach it foes will set on you, who will strain hard to kill you. Be sure that one, or both of you, shall there seal the faith you

hold with blood; but be brave and true till death, and the King will give you a crown of life.

The one who shall die there, though his death will be strange and his pain great, shall have the best of it. He will reach the Ce-les-ti-al Ci-ty first, and rid him self of much woe, which his friend must meet with in the rest of the Way. But when you reach the town, and these things come to pass, then think of your Friend, and quit you like men, and trust your souls to God.

Now I saw in my dream that soon Chris-tian and Faith-ful saw a town in front of them, and the name of that town is Van-i-ty, and at that town there is a Fair kept, named Van-i-ty Fair. It is kept there all the year long, and all that is bought or sold there is vain and void of worth. At this Fair are sold all kinds of things as homes, lands, trades, fame, realms, and all sorts of things to fill the flesh with joy as lusts, wives, lives, souls, gold, pearls, gem stones, and what not. There, too, to be seen at all times are games, plays, fools, apes, knaves, and rogues. Yet he that will go to the Ce-les-ti-al Ci-ty must needs pass through this Fair.

Thus Chris-tian and Faith-ful came to this town and Fair, and all the folk at the Fair made a great stir. A crowd drew 'round them, and some said they had lost their wits, to dress and speak as they did, and 'cause they set no store by the choice goods for sale in Van-i-ty Fair. One of the men of the Fair said to them, What will you buy? But they said to him, We buy the truth. But these words drew from these folks fierce taunts and jeers, and soon the noise and stir grew to such a height that the Great One of the Fair sent his friends to take up these two strange men, and he told them to tell him whence they came, where they went, and what they did there in such a garb?

Chris-tian and Faith-ful told them that they were Pil-grims on the Way to the Ce-les-ti-al Ci-ty; but those who sat to judge the case thought that they must be mad, or else that they had come to stir up strife at the Fair; so they beat them, smeared them with dirt, and put them in a cage, that they might be a sight for all the men at the Fair. There they lay for some time, the butt of scorn and rage to all who went by, and the Lord of the Fair made sport of all that was done to them. But the men

CHRISTIAN & FAITHFULL Pass Through VANITY FAIR

were meek, and gave good words for bad, and kind deeds for blows, so that some of those who saw them (whose eyes were more sharp than the rest) found fault with the more base for their ill use of Chris-tian and Faith-ful.

At which these bad men let fly their rage at those who did plead for them, and said they were of the same sort as the men in the cage, and ought to share their fate. But, said they, these men seem to be men of peace, and to mean no harm, and there are not a few who trade at our Fair who have more need to be put in the cage, and to be sent to jail, too, than these men. When there had been much talk like this on both sides (through all of which Chris-tian and Faith-ful bore up like wise, true men), they fell to blows twixt them selves, and much harm came of it.

Then these two poor men were made to bear all the blame of this brawl. They beat them, put them in chains and led them up and down the Fair, so that none might dare plead for them or join them. But Chris-tian and Faith-ful bore all this spite so well that it won to their side some of the men of the Fair. This made their foes rage the more, so that they swore the pair should die. So they put them in the cage once more and made their feet fast in the stocks.

All this brought to mind what E-van-gel-ist had said would be their fate, and that his lot would be best who would be put to death, so the wish of each was that he might be the one to die. But they left the choice to God, who rules all things, and their souls were full of peace.

At the set time they were brought in to face the court. The name of the judge was Lord Hate-Good. The charge brought was this: That they were foes to the trades of those who sold at Van-i-ty Fair; that they were the cause of the brawls in the town, and had won some at the Fair to their own bad ways, all to spite the Law of their Prince.

Faith-ful said to the judge: As to the brawls you speak of, I did not start them, as I am a man of peace. I did but set my self at that which was 'gainst the true God. As to the Prince you speak of, since he is Be-el-ze-bub, I hold him in scorn. Those who were won to our side, were won by the truth of our words and lives.

Then the judge said, Let those who have aught to say for their Lord the Prince 'gainst this man come and now speak. So three men, whose names were En-vy, Su-per-sti-tion, and Pick-thank, stood forth and swore to speak the truth, and tell what they knew of Faith-ful. En-vy said: My Lord, I have known this man Faith-ful for a long time. He is one of the most vile men in our town. He cares naught for kings or laws, but seeks to spread his own views, and to teach men what he calls faith. I heard him say, That Chris-ti-an-i-ty and the ways of our town were not the same way, and could not be at peace. And does he not when he says such things, speak ill of all our deeds and us as well?

Then Su-per-sti-tion said: My Lord, I know not much of this man, and have no wish to know more; but of this I am sure, that he is a foul man, for he says that our creeds are vain and such by which a man could by no means please God.

Pick-thank was then bid to say what he knew, and his speech ran thus: — My Lord, I have known this man for a long time, and have heard him say things that ought not to be said. He rails at our great Prince Be-el-ze-bub, and says that if all men were of his mind, that prince should no more hold sway. More than this, he hath been heard to rail on you, my Lord, who are now his judge.

Then said the judge to Faith-ful: You base man! Turn coat! Have you heard what these good folk have said of you?

FAITH-FUL. May I speak a few words in my own cause?

JUDGE. Wretch that you are, you have no right to live, but should be slain on the spot; yet, that all men may see how fair we treat you, let us hear what you have to say.

FAITH-FUL. I say then to Envy, That all rules, laws, ways, or men which are flat 'gainst the Word of God are 'gainst Chris-ti-an-i-ty too. If I am wrong in this, show me and I will change my words.

To Su-per-sti-tion I said this, To come to God and praise Him one must have a faith which comes from God and is one with the will of God.

To Pick-Thank I say, That the Prince of this town, and all those who stand with him, are more fit to be in Hell than in this town. And so, I pray the Lord to help me.

Then the judge, to sum up the case to the Ju-ry, spoke thus: You see this man who has made such a stir in our town. You have heard what these good men have said of him, which he owns to be true. It rests now with you to save his life or hang him. But you see that he scorns our faith, and owns to base acts for which he ought to die the death.

Then the Ju-ry went out, whose names were Mr. Blind-Man, Mr. No-Good, Mr. Mal-ice, Mr. Love-Lust, Mr. Live-Loose, Mr. Head-y, Mr. High-Mind, Mr. En-mi-ty, Mr. Li-ar, Mr. Cru-el-ty, Mr. Hate-Light, and Mr. Im-plac-a-ble, and each one gave his voice to the case thus: I can see with a clear eye that this man is full of schisms, said Mr. Blind-Man. Out of the world with him, said Mr. No-Good. I hate the mere look of him, said Mr. Mal-ice. From the first I could not bear him, said Mr. Love-Lust. Nor I, for he would be sure to blame my ways, said Mr. Live-Loose. Hang him, hang him! said Mr. Head-y. A low wretch! said Mr. High-Mind. My heart does rise 'gainst him, said Mr. En-mi-ty. He is a rogue, said Mr. Li-ar. To hang is too good for him, said Mr. Cru-el-ty. Let us kill him, that he may be out of our way, said Mr. Hate-Light. Then said Mr. Im-plac-a-ble: Not to gain all the world would I make peace with him, so let us doom him to death. And so they did, and in a short time he was led back to the place from whence he came, there to be put to the worst death that could be thought of: For first they did scourge him, then they threw stones at him, did prick him with swords, and then burnt him at the stake. Thus did Faith-ful come to his end.

Now I saw that there stood in back of the mob, Hors-es of Light to wait for Faith-ful, and as soon as his foes had put him to death, they bore him up through the clouds, with sound of trump, to the Gate of the Ce-les-ti-al Ci-ty.

But as for Chris-tian, he was led back to his cell, and there staid for a time. But He who rules all things and who had the strength of their rage in His own hand, brought it to pass that Chris-tian, for that time, got free from them and went his way.

Now I saw in my dream that Chris-tian did not go forth by him self. One whose name was Hope-ful—made such by the words and deeds of Faith-ful and Chris-tian in Van-i-ty Fair—told him that he would go with him. He said, too, that not a few of the men of the Fair would do the same thing in time.

FAITHFUL SUFFERS DEATH at VANITY FAIR

H C Selous

So I saw that just as they got out of the Fair, they saw a man on the road whom they caught up to, whose name was By-Ends*. So they did ask him: What town are you from? How far do you go this way? Then he told them that he came from the town of Fair-Speech and was on his way to the Ce-les-ti-al Ci-ty (but he did not tell them his name).

CHRIS-TIAN. Are there any good men who live in Fair-Speech?

BY-ENDS. Yes, I hope.

CHRIS-TIAN. Pray, sir, what may I call you?

BY-ENDS. You do not know me, but if you go this way, I shall be glad to have you join me.

CHRIS-TIAN. This town of Fair-Speech, I have heard that it is a place where most there are rich men.

BY-ENDS. Yes. That it is. My kin folk who live there are rich.

CHRIS-TIAN. Pray, who are your kin folk?

BY-ENDS. Near the whole town. As my Lord Turn-A-bout, my Lord Time-Ser-ver, my Lord Fair-Speech (from whose kin folk the town was named), Mr. Smooth-Man, Mr. Fac-ing-Both-Ways, and Rev. Two-Tongues. To tell you the truth, I am a well to do man, though my great grand pa was but a boat man, who did row one way, but did not look the same way.

CHRIS-TIAN. Do you have a wife?

BY-ENDS. Yes, my wife is quite well bred, too. Her ma ma was my La-dy Feign-ing. 'Tis true, our creeds are not like those who are strict, but in two small points: First, we do not strive 'gainst wind and tide. Next, We are most full of zeal when Chris-ti-an-i-ty goes in plush clothes; we love to walk with Chris-tians in the street, if the sun shines and men clap their hands to praise them.

Then Chris-tian stept near to Hope-ful and said, It runs in my mind that this is one By-Ends of Fair-Speech; and if so, we have as great a knave with us as lives in all these parts. Then

---

* Mr. By-Ends represents those whose religious profession is a cover for their covetousness, worldly lusts, and selfish ambitions. By-Ends is determined to achieve his end purpose of living richly and well by any means he can. This includes his being religious when, as he says, "Religion goes in silver slippers...if the sun shines, and the people applaud." By-Ends is quite proud of the luxury of his home town and the eminence of his relatives, yet he is ashamed of his name, for men do not want the mask of their religious profession removed to reveal their true covetous motivations beneath.

Hope-ful said, Ask him his name. So Chris-tian came up with him and said, Is not your name By-Ends of Fair Speech?

BY-ENDS. That is not my name, but a nick name that those who do not like me call me.

CHRIS-TIAN. Did not those who call you this, do so 'cause of the life you live?

BY-ENDS. No! No! I have just had the luck to jump in with the times, be what they were, if it was my chance to gain there by.

CHRIS-TIAN. I thought you were the man. I fear this name sticks to you more so than you would like to say.

BY-ENDS. I will be a fair friend to you if you will let me come with you.

CHRIS-TIAN. If you go with us, you must go 'gainst wind and tide, which you will not like. You must be a Chris-tian in rags as well as in plush clothes; and stand firm when Chris-tians are bound in chains, as well as when they walk the streets and men clap their hands to praise them.

BY-ENDS. You must not tell me how I will live. Leave me to be free and to do what I wish and I will go with you.

CHRIS-TIAN. Not one step more, till you say you will stand with us in the way I spoke to you of.

BY-ENDS. I will not leave my creeds, since they do no harm and help me to get gain. If I may not go with you, leave me to my self, till some come by who will be glad to walk with me.

Now I saw in my dream that Chris-tian and Hope-ful left him and did walk on first. Then one of them did look back and saw three men come up to Mr. By-Ends and he did bow to them and they did praise him. The names of these men were Mr. Hold-the-World*, Mr. Mon-ey Love*, and Mr. Save-All*, men

---

* Mr. Hold-the-World thinks he has found the secret of doing what Christ says no man can do, "No man can serve two masters: for either he will hate the one, and love the other; or else he will hold to the one, and despise the other. Ye cannot serve God and mammon" (Matthew 6:24). In reality, Mr. Hold-the-World's name reveals clearly what he holds to, therefore he must of consequence, despise the true religion of Christian and Faithful, calling them "fools."

* Mr. Money-Love thinks it is consistent with godliness for a minister to change his principles in order to get a more lucrative position or for a tradesman to become religious to gain a rich wife or secure more customers for his business. Like many in the church in our day, his end is to gain wealth for himself and his religion is a stalking-horse to help him get it. He is like those mentioned by Paul in his letter to Timothy: "In the last days...men shall be lovers of their own selves, covetous" (II Timothy 3:1, 2).

that Mr. By-Ends knew when they were youths in the town of Love-Gain. There they had learnt how to get much for them selves and how to lie, cheat, praise men, and put on the cloak of Chris-ti-an-i-ty to gain wealth. These men did ask 'bout Chris-tian and Hope-ful and By-Ends told them of all their talk.

Then did Mr. By-Ends ask the men if it were right for a man to change his creed if it would cause him to get much gain by it. To this Mr. Mon-ey-Love did speak and his talk did please all of them. And since they thought all men could do naught but praise him for what he said, they did call to Chris-tian and Hope-ful to hear what they would say to this. At their call Chris-tian and Hope-ful stopt and stood still to wait for them, but the men thought it best that Mr. Hold-the-World ask this of them, not Mr. By-Ends, to whom they did talk with at first.

So they came up to Chris-tian and Hope-ful and did ask them if they thought it right for a man to change his creed if he could get great gain by it.

Then Chris-tian said, If it is 'gainst the Word of God to come after Christ just for bread and fish, as it is in John 6, how much worse is it to use Christ and Chris-ti-an-i-ty to gain the world and the things in it? None but Pa-gans, Dev-ils, Hy-po-crites, and Witch-es are of this creed.

The Phar-i-sees were of this creed, who did pray a long time, but sought to gain the homes of the poor by their craft (Luke 20:46-47). Ju-das the Dev-il was of this creed, too. He did right with a false heart to gain the coins in the bag so he could be rich, but he was lost and cast from God, a Son of Hell. Si-mon the Witch was of his creed, who would have the Ho-ly Spir-it to gain wealth for him self (Acts 8:19-22).

Thus we see that the man who takes up Chris-ti-an-i-ty for the world, will cast Chris-ti-an-i-ty from him for the world, too. Ju-das did come to Christ for the things of the world, so he did sell the Lord for his love of the world. To say that a man may change his creed to gain the things of the world, as I think you have done, is to be a Pa-gan, an Hy-po-crite, and a Dev-il, and at the last day your pay will be as your works have been.

---

* Mr. Save-All's name implies that he believes that all professors of Christianity will be saved in the end, no matter how they live now. He does not like those who have convictions about holiness and righteous living being a necessity for the true convert, referring to such people as rigid and judgmental.

Mr. Money-Love's Lesson in Hypocrisy.

Then did Mr. By-Ends, Mr. Hold-the-World, Mr. Save-All, and Mr. Mon-ey-Love all stare with a blank face, for they knew not what to say. So Mr. By-Ends and his friends did halt and kept back from Chris-tian and Hope-ful so that they would out go them.

Then did Chris-tian say to Hope-ful, If these men are mute when dealt with by a mere man, what will they do when they face God and see the fires of Hell?

So Chris-tian and Hope-ful out went them and came to a plain called Ease, but they went through it at a fast pace. Now past the plain was a small hill called Lu-cre, and in that hill a Sil-ver Mine, which some had in past times gone to see, but they had come too near the edge of the pit and the ground had broke, and they were slain by their fall.

Then I saw in my dream, that a bit off the road, next to the Sil-ver Mine, stood De-mas* who did call to Chris-tian and Hope-ful: Ho! Come here and I will show you a thing.

CHRIS-TIAN. What thing so great as to turn us from the Way?

DE-MAS. Here is a Sil-ver Mine and with some pain to dig, you can be rich.

HOPE-FUL. Let us go see.

CHRIS-TIAN. Not I, for I have heard of this place, and how some have been slain here. Wealth is a snare to those who seek it.

Then Chris-tian did say to De-mas, Is not the place full of snares?

DE-MAS. Not so, but just to those who take no care of them selves, but he did blush as he spoke.

CHRIS-TIAN. Let us not stir a step to it, but still keep in the Way.

HOPE-FUL. I will bet when By-Ends comes here, he will turn to look at it.

---

* Demas is named for the companion of the Apostle, who deserted Paul because he loved this present world more than God. Here his namesake in Bunyan's allegory stands by a silver mine to lure unsuspecting Pilgrims to their deaths, even as the love of money has ruined many promising professors of faith in Christ who do not heed the advice of the Apostle that those "that will be rich fall into temptation and a snare, and into many foolish and hurtful lusts, which drown men in destruction and perdition" (I Timothy 6:9). Note that Christian will not even take one step out of the Way to look at the tempting sight (Proverbs 1:10), and instead faithfully rebukes Demas for his treachery.

DEMAS
tempts CHRISTIAN and HOPEFUL

CHRIS-TIAN. No doubt of it, for his creed leads him that way. I would guess, too, that he will die there.

DE-MAS. But will you not come and see? I too am of your creed and if you will stop for a while, I will go on with you.

CHRIS-TIAN. What is your name? Is it not De-mas?

DE-MAS. Yes, my name is De-mas. I am a son of A-bra-ham.

CHRIS-TIAN. I know you, De-mas. Ga-ha-zi was just like you and Ju-das was, too. You have trod in their steps, but you use a trick to lure us. Ju-das was hanged for his sin and you will get no less for yours. When we see the King, we will tell him of your works. Thus they went on their Way.

By this time By-Ends and his friends were come in their sight, and they at the first beck went to De-mas. Now it may be that they fell in the pit, or they went down to dig and did not come out, of these things I know not, but I do know that they were not seen in the Way at all, for all time.

Now I saw that just on the back side of this plain, Chris-tian and Hope-ful came to an Old Mon-u-ment by the side of the high way and did stop to look at it. It did seem to them to be the form of a girl, but was now like stone. This they saw on it: Call to Mind Lot's Wife. So they thought this must be where God did change Lot's wife to a block of salt, for she did look back at So-dom with lust in her heart for it.

CHRIS-TIAN. Ah, my good Hope-ful! We might have both been like this had we gone to De-mas to look at the Sil-ver Mine at the hill Lu-cre.

HOPE-FUL. What a fool I was! She did but look back, but I, in my heart, did want to go see. The sight of this Mon-u-ment should cause us to shun her sin, or else we may be made like her. So let us Call to Mind Lot's Wife and thank God and fear Him.

Then Chris-tian and Hope-ful went on till they came to a fair stream, which Da-vid calls the Riv-er of God, but John the Riv-er of the Wa-ter of Life. Now their Way lay just on the bank of this stream, and here they found good cheer. They drank from the stream, which gave them new strength. On its banks, on each side, were green trees with all kinds of fruits; and they ate the leaves to cool their blood, and heal all their ails. On each side of the stream was a field all in sweet bloom, and it was green all the year long. In this field they lay down and slept, for here they were safe.

When they woke, they ate once more of the fruit of the trees, and drank from the stream, and then lay down to sleep. So they did for some days and nights, and then they ate and drank, and set out once more on the Way, for they were not yet at its end.

Now I saw in my dream that they had not gone far when their path left the bank of the stream for a time, at which they were sad, yet they did not go out of the Way.

Now the Way grew rough, and their feet were sore from their long march, and their souls were much cast down from these things. So, they did wish for a way of ease. Now on the left hand of the road was By-Path Mea-dow, a fair green field with a path

The Pillar of Salt.

H.C.Selous.   W.THOMAS. Sc.

through it, and too, a stile which they must go past to get to the Mea-dow. Come, good Hope-ful, said Chris-tian, let us go past the stile and walk on the grass.

HOPE-FUL. But what if this path should lead us out of the Way?

CHRIS-TIAN. How can it? Look, does it not go side by side with it?

So they went past the stile and got to the Path. Here they found it good for their feet. But they had not gone far when they saw in front of them a man, whose name was Vain-Con-fi-dence, so they did ask him which way the path led and he said, To the Ce-les-ti-al Ci-ty. Did I not tell you so? said Chris-tian. So the man went on in front of them; but lo, the night came on, and it grew so dark that they lost sight of their guide, Vain-Con-fi-dence, who as he did not see the path in front of him, fell in a deep pit, put there by the Prince to catch vain fools, and he was slain in his fall. And Chris-tian and Hope-ful heard him fall.

HOPE-FUL. Where are we now? said Hope-ful.

Then was Chris-tian mute, as he thought he had led his friend out of the way. And now light was seen to flash from the sky, and rain came down in streams.

HOPE-FUL (with a groan). Oh, that I had kept on the Way!

CHRIS-TIAN. Who could have thought that this path should lead us out of our Way?

HOPE-FUL. I had my fears from the first, and so gave you a hint. I would have been more plain with you had I been as old as you.

CHRIS-TIAN. Good Hope-ful, let what I have done not hurt the way you think of me. It is a great grief to me that I have brought you out of the Way. Trust me, that I did not mean to do it.

HOPE-FUL. I do, my friend, and I have faith that this shall be for our good.

CHRIS-TIAN. I am glad I have such a kind friend with me; but we must not stand here; let us try to get back.

HOPE-FUL. But, good friend, let me go first.

CHRIS-TIAN. No, if you please, let me go first, so if there be risk, I may meet it first, for by my fault we have both gone out of the Way.

No, said Hope-ful, you shall not go first, for your mind is not at rest, and you may lead us wrong once more.

Then they heard a voice say: Set thine heart to the high way, the way thou hast been; turn once more. But by this time the stream was deep from the rain that fell, and to get back did not seem safe; yet they went back, though it was so dark and the stream ran so high that nine or ten times, it was like to drown them. Nor could they, with all their skill, get back that night to the stile. So they found a shield from the rain, and there they slept till break of day.

Now, not far from the place where they lay was Doubt-ing Cas-tle, the lord of which was Gi-ant De-spair; and it was on his ground that they now slept. There Gi-ant De-spair found them, and with a gruff voice he bade them wake. Where do you go? said he; and What brought you here? They told him they were Pil-grims and that they had lost their Way. Then said Gi-ant De-spair: You have no right to come in here on these grounds; the land on which you lie is mine.

So they were made to go by force, since he had much more strength than they did. Nor did they have much to say, as they knew they were at fault. So Gi-ant Despair drove them on, and put them in a dark and foul cell in the Dun-geon of the Cas-tle. Here they were kept for more than three days, and they had no light nor food, nor a drop to drink all that time, and no one to ask them how they did. They were in a sad state, and far from all friends, but Chris-tian's grief was made twice as great by the thought it had all come through his wrong course.

Now Gi-ant De-spair had a wife, whose name was Dif-fi-dence, and he told her what he had done. Then he said, What shall I do with them? Beat them well, said his wife. So when he rose he took a stout stick from a crab tree, and went down to the cell where poor Chris-tian and Hope-ful lay, and beat them as if they were dogs, so that they could not turn on the floor; and they spent all that day in sighs and tears.

The next day he came once more, and found them sore from the stripes, and said that since there was no chance for them to be let out of the cell, their best way would be to put an end to their own lives with knife or rope. For why should you wish to live, he said, with all this woe? But they told him they did hope he would let them go. With that he sprang up with a fierce look, and no doubt would have made an end of them him self, but that he fell in one of his fits for a time (for some times in sun shine he fell in fits), and for a time, lost the use of his hand; so he drew back, and left them to think of what he had said.

CHRIS-TIAN. Friend, what shall we do? The life that we now lead is worse than death. For my part I know not which is best, to live thus, or to die out of hand, as I feel that the grave would be less sad to me than this Dun-geon. Shall we let Gi-ant De-spair rule us?

HOPE-FUL. In a good truth our case is a sad one, and to die would be more sweet to me than to live here; yet let us bear in mind that the Lord of that land to which we go hath said: Thou shalt not kill. And for one to kill him self is to kill both flesh and soul at once. My friend Chris-tian, you talk of ease in the grave, but must not a man who takes his own life go to Hell? All the law is not in the hands of Gi-ant De-spair.

Who knows but that God, who made the world, may cause him to die, or he may not lock us in, or lose the use of his limbs as he did at first. I have made up my mind to pluck up the heart of a man, and to try to get out of this strait. Fool that I was not to do so when first he came to the Dun-geon, but let us not put an end to our own lives, for a good time to get out may come yet.

By these words did Hope-ful soothe his friend, and change the tone of Chris-tian's mind.

Well, at night the Gi-ant went down to the Dun-geon to see if life was still in them, and in good truth, that life was just in them was all that could be said, for from their wounds and lack of food they did no more than just breathe. When Gi-ant De-spair found they were not dead, he fell in a great rage, and said that since they had not done what he had told them to do (kill them selves), it should be worse with them than if they had not been born.

At this they shook with fear, and Chris-tian fell down in a swoon; but when he came to, Hope-ful said, My friend, call to mind how strong in faith you have been till now. A-pol-lyon could not crush you, nor could all that you heard, or saw, or felt in the Val-ley of the Shad-ow of Death. Look at the fears, the griefs, the woes that you have gone through. Are you now full of fear? I, too, am in this Dun-geon, far more weak a man

Christian & Hopeful in the Castle of Giant Despair

than you, and Gi-ant De-spair dealt his blows at me as well as you, and keeps me from food, drink, and light. Let us both (if but to shun the shame) bear up as well as we can, and wait the Lord's will.

When night came on, the wife of Gi-ant De-spair said to him: Well, will the two men yield? To which he said: No, they are stout rogues; they choose to bear all, and will not put an end to their lives. Then she said: At dawn of day take them to the yard, and show them where the skulls and bones of all those whom you have put to death have been thrown, and make them think you will tear them up, and kill them as well.

So Gi-ant De-spair took them to the Cas-tle Yard, and said: These men were like you, and they were caught on my grounds as you were, and when I saw fit I tore them in shreds. In ten days' time you shall be thrown in here if you do not yield. Go—get you down to your den once more. With that he beat them all the way back, and there they lay the whole day in a sad plight.

Now, when night was come, Dif-fi-dence said to the Gi-ant: I fear much that these men live on in hopes to pick the lock of the cell and get free. Do you think so, my dear? said Gi-ant De-spair. Then at sun rise I will search them.

Now, late that night, as Chris-tian and Hope-ful lay in the den, they fell on their knees to pray, and knelt till the day broke; when Chris-tian gave a start, and said: Fool that I am thus to lie in this dark Dun-geon when I might walk at large! I have a key in my pouch, the name of which is Prom-ise, that I feel sure, will turn the locks of all the doors in Doubt-ing Cas-tle. Then said Hope-ful: That is good news; pluck it from your breast, and let us try it.

So when Chris-tian put the key in the lock, the bolt sprang back, and the door flew wide with ease, and Chris-tian and Hope-ful both came out. When they got to the the door that leads to the Cas-tle Yard the key did just as well; but the lock of the last strong gate of Doubt-ing Castle was hard to turn, yet the key did turn it at last, but the hinge gave so loud a creak that it woke up Gi-ant De-spair, who sprang up to catch them. But just then he felt his limbs fail, for a fit came on him, so that he could by no means go to catch them.

Chris-tian and Hope-ful now fled back to the high way, and so were safe 'cause they were out of his grounds. Now, when

CRISTIAN HOPEFUL escape from DOUBTING CASTLE

they were gone past the stile, they thought they should warn
those who might chance to come on this road. So they cut
these words on a post: This stile leads to Doubt-ing Cas-tle,
which is kept by Gi-ant De-spair, who hates the King of the Ce-
les-tial Coun-try, and seeks to slay those who are on their way
to his land.

Now quite a few who went that way read these words and
gave heed to them.

Then they came to The De-lect-a-ble Moun-tains, which the
Lord of the Hill owns. Here they saw fruit trees, vines, plants,
shrubs, and streams, and drank and ate of the grapes. Now
there were Shep-herds at the tops of these hills who kept
watch on their flocks. So Chris-tian and Hope-ful went up to

them and as they stood by the high way, they leaned on their staves to rest, while thus they spoke to the Shep-herds, Who owns these De-lect-a-ble Moun-tains? And whose are the sheep that feed on them?

SHEP-HERDS. These hills are Im-man-u-el's, and the sheep are His too, and He laid down his life for them.

CHRIS-TIAN. Is this the way to the Ce-les-ti-al Ci-ty?

SHEP-HERDS. You are on the right road.

CHRIS-TIAN. How far is it?

SHEP-HERDS. Too far for all but those that shall get there, in truth.

CHRIS-TIAN. Is the way safe?

SHEP-HERDS. Safe for those for whom it is meant to be safe; but men of sin shall fall there.

CHRIS-TIAN. Is there a place of rest for those who are tired and faint on the Way?

SHEP-HERDS. The Lord of these Hills gave us a charge to help those that came here, should they be known to us or not; so the good things of the place are yours.

I then saw in my dream that the Shep-herds did ask them: Where have you come from? How did you get in the Way? and, By what means have you got so far? For but few of those that set out to come here do show their face on these hills.

So when Chris-tian and Hope-ful told their tale, it pleased the Shep-herds and they did look with love on Chris-tian and Hope-ful, and said: With joy we greet you on The De-lect-a-ble Moun-tains!

Now the names of the Shep-herds were Know-ledge, Ex-per-i-ence Watch-ful, and Sin-cere, and they brought Chris-tian and Hope-ful to their tents, and told them to eat of that which was there, and they soon went to their rest for the night.

When the morn broke, the Shep-herds woke up Chris-tian and Hope-ful, and took them to a spot whence they saw a good view on all sides. Then said one of the Shep-herds to the rest: Shall we show these Pil-grims some sights which they will stare with awe at? So when they all said, Yes, they took them first to the top of a high hill, the name of which was Er-ror. It was steep on the far off side, and they told them to look down to the foot of it. So Chris-tian and Hope-ful cast their eyes

Christian & Hopeful with the Shepherds of the Delectable Mountains

down, and saw there some men who had lost their lives by a fall from the top. Then Chris-tian said, What does this mean?

SHEP-HERDS. Have you not heard of them that were made to err, for they put their trust in false guides?

CHRIS-TIAN. Yes, I have.

SHEP-HERDS. These are they, and to this day they have not been put in a tomb, but are left here to warn men to take good heed lest they come too near the brink of this ledge.

Then I saw that they had led them to the top of Mount Cau-tion, and bade them look far off. When they did they saw, as they thought, some men walk up and down through the grave stones that were there. And they saw that the men were blind, 'cause they some times did trip on the tombs, and could not get out from that place. What means this? said Chris-tian.

SHEP-HERDS. Did you not see a stile that led to a Mea-dow a short ways 'fore you came to these De-lec-ta-ble Moun-tains?

CHRIS-TIAN AND HOPE-FUL. Yes.

SHEP-HERDS. From that stile there goes a path to Doubt-ing Cas-tle, which is kept by Gi-ant De-spair, and the men whom you see down there came as you do now, till they got up to that stile; and, as the right Way was rough to walk in, they chose to go through the Mea-dow, and there Gi-ant De-spair took them, and shut them up in Doubt-ing Cas-tle, where they were kept in a Dun-geon for a while, till he at last put out their eyes, and led them down there to these tombs, where he left them to walk, trip, and fall, and there they are still. At this Chris-tian gave a look at Hope-ful, and they both burst out with sobs and tears, but yet said not a word.

Then I saw in my dream, that the Shep-herds had them to a place where there was a door in the side of a hill, and they threw back the door and bade the Pil-grims look in. They did so and saw that it was quite dark and full of smoke. There Christian and Hope-ful thought they heard fires burn, the cries of some in great woe, and they smelt the scent of brim stone. Then said Chris-tian, What means this?

SHEP-HERDS. This is a By-Way to Hell. This is where Hy-po-crites go: such as those who are like E-sau, who sold his Birth-right; those who sell their Lord, with Ju-das; those who speak ill of God's Word like Al-ex-an-der; and those who lie and try to cheat men as An-an-i-as and his wife Sap-phi-ra did.

HOPE-FUL. I would bet that each of these had on them the marks of a Pil-grim, as we do now, had they not?

SHEP-HERDS. Yes, and they held it a long time, too.

HOPE-FUL. How far might they go on the Way to the Ce-les-ti-al Ci-ty in their day, since they did end up in Hell?

SHEP-HERDS. Some past these Moun-tains, and some not quite as far.

Then Chris-tian and Hope-ful said, We had need to cry to the strong for strength.

SHEP-HERDS. Ay, and you will have need to use it, when you have it, too.

Then the four Shep-herds took them up a high hill, the name of which was Clear, that they might see the Gates of The Ce-les-tial Ci-ty with the aid of a glass to look through, but their hands shook 'cause of the last thing they had seen, so they could not see well.

When Chris-tian and Hope-ful thought they would move on, one of the Shep-herds gave them a note of the Way. The next told them to Watch Out For the Flat-ter-er, and the third bade them take heed that they slept not on The En-chant-ed Ground, and the fourth bade them God Speed. Now it was that I woke from my dream.

Then I slept, and dreamt once more, and saw Chris-tian and Hope-ful go down near the foot of these hills, where lies the land of Con-ceit, from which land there comes in to the Way, a small lane which winds back and forth. Here they met a brisk lad, whose name was Ig-no-rance*, to whom Chris-tian said: Where do you come from? and To what place do you go?

IG-NO-RANCE. Sir, I was born in the land that lies off there on the left, and I wish to go to The Ce-les-tial Ci-ty.

CHRIS-TIAN. How do you think to get in at the Gate?

IG-NO-RANCE. Just as all good men do.

---

* Ignorance represents those who are puffed up and wise in their own eyes. He comes from the land of Conceit. He thinks he knows much about God and heavenly things, but he does not even know the most basic truths of the Word of God, so he is, like his name, ignorant. He trusts that his own heart is good, and a faithful guide to him. Speaking of spiritual ignorance, David Clarkson says, "Ignorance is spiritual darkness, the very shadow of eternal death. There is but a small portion between you and hell. Hell is outer darkness, and ignorance is inner darkness; it is the very next room to hell" (The Works of David Clarkson, Volume 2, p. 250).

CHRIS-TIAN. But what have you to show at that Gate to pass through it?

IG-NO-RANCE. I know my Lord's will, and I have led a good life; I pay for all that I have, I pray, fast, give tithes, and give alms, and have left my own land for that to which I now go.

CHRIS-TIAN. But you came not in at the Wick-et Gate that is at the head of this Way; you came in through a lane which winds back and forth, so that I fear, though you may think well of all you have done, that when the time shall come, you will have this laid at your charge: That you are a thief—and so you will not get in.

IG-NO-RANCE. Well, I know you not; so keep to your own creed, and I will keep to mine, and I hope all will be well. And as for the Gate that you talk of, all the world knows that it is far from our land, and I do not think that there is a man in all our parts who does so much as know the way to it, and I see not what need there is that he should, since we have, as you see, a fine green lane at the next turn that comes down from our part of the world.

When Chris-tian saw the man was wise in his own self love, he said in a low tone of voice to Hope-ful: There is more hope of a fool than of him. Shall we talk more with him now, or out go him and let him think on what he has heard till now and then stop and talk more, to see if we can do him good that way?

HOPE-FUL. It is not good to talk to him all at once. Let us pass on if you will, and talk to him by and by, when may be, he can bear it.

So they went on, and Ig-no-rance trod in their steps a short way back of them. Soon they came to a dark lane, where they met a man whom Sev-en Dev-ils had bound with strong cords, to take him back to the door they had seen in the side of the hill. Now good Chris-tian did start to shake with fear, and so did Hope-ful. As the Dev-ils led the man off, Chris-tian did look to see if he knew the man; and he thought it might be one Turn-A-way from the town of A-pos-ta-sy. But Chris-tian did not see his whole face, for the man did hang his head like a thief that is caught. As they went past, Hope-ful saw a note on his back which said, Wan-ton Pro-fes-sor and Dam-na-ble A-pos-tate.

They then did go on till they saw a road branch off from the one they were in, and they knew not which of the two to take, for both did seem to go on straight in front of them. As they stood to think of it, a man whose skin was black, but who was clad in a white robe*, came to them and said: Why do you stand here? They told him that they were on their way to the Ce-les-ti-al Ci-ty, but knew not which of the two roads to take.

---

* The Flatterer leads Christian and Hopeful astray little by little, so that in a while their backs are turned away from the Celestial City. The Flatterer is armed with a smooth tongue and eloquent speech flowing from it and appears to the Pilgrims to be like an angel of light, seducing those who follow him into a false peace. We should all heed the words of Solomon, "A man that flattereth his neighbor spreadeth a net for his feet" (Proverbs 29:5), lest we be beguiled by those who would puff up the self-love that remains in us and massage our egos to gain what they want from us and lead us astray, too.

Come with me then, said the man, for it is there that I mean to go. So they went with him, a short ways back of him, yet they did not see that bit by bit the road did turn, so that soon they could not see the Ci-ty they were on the way to. By and by, the man led them both in to a net, in which they were caught and knew not what to do. Then the white robe fell off the black man's back, and they saw where they were. So they lay down and wept for some time, for they could not get out of the net.

CHRIS-TIAN. I have been wrong. Did not the Shep-herds tell us to Watch Out For the Flat-ter-er? And the Wise Man wrote, The man who is a Flat-ter-er doth spread a net for your feet.

HOPE-FUL. Those Shep-herds, too, gave us a note of the way, but we have not read it, and so have not kept in the right path. Thus they lay in the net to weep and wail.

At last they saw a Bright One come up to them with a whip of fine cord in his hand, who said: Where are you going? What do you do here?

They told him that their wish was to go to Zi-on, but that they had been led out of the Way by a black man with a white cloak on, who said he was bound for the same place and that he would show them the road.

Then the man with the whip said: It is Flat-ter-er, a false man, who has put on the garb of an An-gel of Light for a time. So he cut the net and let the men out. And he told them to come with him, that he might set them in the right Way once more. Then he said: Where were you last night?

CHRIS-TIAN AND HOPE-FUL. With the Shep-herds who kept watch on their sheep on The De-lec-ta-ble Moun-tains.

BRIGHT ONE. Did not the Shep-herds give you a note of the Way?

CHRIS-TIAN AND HOPE-FUL. Yes.

BRIGHT ONE. But when you were at a stand why did you not read your note?

They told him they had not thought of it.

BRIGHT ONE. Did not the Shep-herds tell you to Watch Out For the Flat-ter-er?

They said, Yes, but we did not think this man, who spoke so fine, was he.

Now I saw in my dream that he bade them lie down, and when they did so he did whip them sore, to teach them the good way in which they should walk. And he said: Those whom I love, I chide and flog, so grieve and mourn and learn from your sin. So they gave him thanks for what he had taught them, and went on the right Way up the hill with a song of joy.

Now in a short while, they saw far off, one by him self, come to meet them. Then said Chris-tian, There is a man with his back to Mount Zi-on, and he does come at us.

HOPE-FUL. Let us take heed, lest he too prove like Flat-ter-er.

So he drew near and at last came up to them. His name was A-the-ist*, and he asked them where they did go.

CHRIS-TIAN. We are on our way to Mount Zi-on.

Then did A-the-ist laugh and laugh.

CHRIS-TIAN. Why do you laugh?

A-THE-IST. I laugh to see how dumb you are, to come on such a hard trip, and yet are like to get naught for your pains.

CHRIS-TIAN. Why, man? Do you think we shall not be let in?

A-THE-IST. Let in! There is no such place as you dream of in all this world.

CHRIS-TIAN. But there is in the world to come.

A-THE-IST. When I was in my home town, I heard of Mount Zi-on, and went out to find it, and have sought it for twice ten years, but I have found no more of it now than the first day I set out.

CHRIS-TIAN. We have both heard and have faith that there is such a place to be found.

A-THE-IST. When at home, I too had faith, else I had not come so far to seek it. But I have found no such place and I have out gone you by a long ways. Now I do go back to my town, and will seek joy in those things that I then cast from me. For there is no such place as Mount Zi-on.

---

* Atheist is a man who scoffs at Christianity and laughs at Christian and Hopeful for believing that there is any heaven to be found. Whatever faith he may have had at the beginning was a dead faith (John 2:23-25; James 2:19) and his heart, having never been changed, inclines him back to the pleasures of the world. He believes only in what he can see, but his mind and spiritual understanding have been blinded by the god of this world (II Corinthians 4:3-4), that he might not see the glory of Christ.

CHRISTIAN AND HOPEFUL
MEET WITH ATHEIST

CHRIS-TIAN. Then Chris-tian said to Hope-ful, Is it true what this man says?

HOPE-FUL. Take heed to your self. He is one of the Flat-ter-ers. What! No Mount Zi-on? Did we not see the Gate of the Ci-ty from the De-lec-ta-ble Moun-tains? Are we not now to walk by faith? Let us go on, lest the man with the whip catch up to us once more.

CHRIS-TIAN. Now I see the truth in your heart, for I did not ask this 'cause I did doubt, but to prove you. This man is made blind by the God of this world. Let us go on, for we have faith in the truth, and we know that no lie is of the truth.

So they did turn their backs on A-the-ist and he did laugh more at them, and went on his way.

At length they came to a land the air of which made men sleep, and here Hope-ful's mind grew dull, and he said: I am so tired. Let us lie down here and take a nap.

CHRIS-TIAN. By no means, lest if we sleep we wake no more.

HOPE-FUL. Why, friend Chris-tian? Sleep is sweet to the man who has spent the day in toil.

CHRIS-TIAN. Do you not call to mind that one of the Shep-herds bade us to watch out for the En-chant-ed Ground? He meant by that that we should take heed not to sleep; so let us not sleep, but watch.

HOPE-FUL. I see I am in fault. Had I been here by my self, my sleep might have been to death.

CHRIS-TIAN. Now then, to keep sleep from our eyes I will ask you, as we go, to tell me how you came at first to do as you do now?

HOPE-FUL. Do you mean how came I first to look to the good of my soul?

CHRIS-TIAN. Yes, that is what I mean.

HOPE-FUL. For a long time the things that were seen and sold at Van-i-ty Fair were a great joy to me.

CHRIS-TIAN. What things do you speak of?

HOPE-FUL. All the good and rich things of this world, I too, took joy in: such things as lies, oaths, strong drink, and lewd things; nor did I keep the Lord's day, in a word, I did prize love of self and all that tends to kill the soul. But I heard from you and Faith-ful that the end of these things is death. And that for these things the wrath of God does come on men.

CHRIS-TIAN. Did you then start to see that your sins were vile?

HOPE-FUL. No, I did not want to see my sins as vile, nor that they would send me to Hell. So, when I heard the Word of God, I did try to shut my eyes at my sins.

CHRIS-TIAN. Then did you at some times get rid of these thoughts of grief?

HOPE-FUL. Yes, for sin was yet sweet to my flesh and I did not want to leave it, and the hours in which my sins came to mind made me sad, and I could not bear it. Thus these thoughts would some times leave me, but then they would come back with more strength.

BEWARE of SLEEPING on the ENCHANTED GROUND.

JHCSelous.

CHRIS-TIAN. And what was it that brought the thoughts of your sins back to mind?

HOPE-FUL. Much! As,

1. If I did but meet a good man in the streets; or,
2. If I heard the Bi-ble read; or,
3. If my head did start to ache; or,
4. If I was told a friend was sick; or,
5. If I heard the bell ring for the dead; or,
6. When I thought of my own death; or,
7. If I heard of the swift death of some one else; or,
8. Most of all, when I thought that I must one day stand in front of God as my judge.

CHRIS-TIAN. And could you, with ease, throw off these thoughts and the guilt of your sin when they came to you?

HOPE-FUL. No, for then these thoughts did stir up the sense of right and wrong with in me, so if I did think to go back to my sins, it was twice as much pain to me.

CHRIS-TIAN. What did you do then?

HOPE-FUL. I did try to clean up my life, but that did not help for long. These words came to me: All our good deeds are like mire and dirt. By the works of the Law, no man shall be saved. When you have done all things, say, We are vain. I could not tell what to do, till I spoke to Faith-ful, for he and I were friends. He told me that my own good deeds done to the end of time could not help me, and that none but a man who had not sinned could save me.

CHRIS-TIAN. Did you ask him, What man this was?

HOPE-FUL. Yes, and he told me it was the Lord Je-sus who now dwells at the right hand of the Most High God, that by what He did in the days of His flesh and, too, when he did hang on the cross, through Him a man could be freed from sin. He told me to beg God the Fa-ther with all my heart and soul to give me light and show the Lord Je-sus to me.

CHRIS-TIAN. And did you do as you were told?

HOPE-FUL. Yes, once, twice, and more.

CHRIS-TIAN. Did the Father then show the Lord Je-sus to you?

HOPE-FUL. Not the first, nor the next, nor the third, nor the fourth, nor the fifth, nor the sixth time.

CHRIS-TIAN. What did you do then?

HOPE-FUL. I could not tell what to do.

CHRIS-TIAN. Did you think to stop your prayers?

HOPE-FUL. Yes, yes, yes.

CHRIS-TIAN. Why did you not do so?

HOPE-FUL. I did think what he had told me was the truth, that is, that not a thing in all the world could not save me, but just Christ and the worth of His pure life lived on earth and His death on the cross to pay in full my debt of sin. Thus I thought, if I quit, I die and go to Hell; but if I do not quit, I can but die at the Throne of Grace. So I kept up prayer till the Father did show His Son to me.

CHRIS-TIAN. And how did He show Him to you?

HOPE-FUL. I did not see Him with my eyes, but in my mind and heart. One day I was quite sad, through a fresh sight of how vile I was and how great were my sins. I saw how much I was fit for Hell and my soul to be cast off for ever. Then out of the blue these words came to me, as if from Christ Him self, Have true faith in the Lord Je-sus Christ, and you will be saved. And I said, Lord my sins are so great, may such a vile man of sin be saved by Thee? Then I, as it were, heard Him say, He that comes to Me, I will in no way cast out; and, Je-sus Christ came to the world to save those who know they are vile; and, He is the end for those who try in vain to keep the Law to be saved and turn to Him for all; and, He died for our sins and rose up to make us right in front of God; and, He did wash us from our sins by His own blood. From all these things I thought, I must look just to Him, His pure life on earth charged to me, His blood shed for me, and this and just this to be saved. And now was my heart filled with joy, my eyes full of tears with love to Je-sus Christ.

CHRIS-TIAN. Of a truth, by this the Fa-ther did show you His Son.

HOPE-FUL. Yes, it did show me that all the world stood full of guilt in front of God; it made me full of shame for my sins; it made me love a pure life; it made me want to do all for Je-sus Christ, yea, die for Him, too.

Then I saw in my dream that Hope-ful did look back and saw Ig-no-rance come up in back of them, and he said, Let us wait for him. So they did. Then Chris-tian said to him, Come man, why do you stay so far back?

IG-NO-RANCE. I like much to be by my self.

CHRIS-TIAN. How stands it 'tween your soul and God now?

IG-NO-RANCE. I hope well, for I think of God and Hea-ven.

CHRIS-TIAN. So do De-vils and those in Hell.

IG-NO-RANCE. But I think of them, and want them.

CHRIS-TIAN. So do most who will not come to Hea-ven at all.

IG-NO-RANCE. But I think of them, and leave all for them.

CHRIS-TIAN. That I doubt, for to leave all is a hard thing. Why do you think you leave all for them?

IG-NO-RANCE. My heart tells me so.

CHRIS-TIAN. The wise man says, He that trusts in his own heart, is a fool.

IGNORANCE STEPS BEHIND

IG-NO-RANCE. That is said of a bad heart, but mine is good.

CHRIS-TIAN. How do you prove that?

IG-NO-RANCE. My heart is at rest in hopes of Hea-ven.

CHRIS-TIAN. That may be a trick of your own heart. Men may rest in hopes of Hea-ven, but have no ground to do so.

IG-NO-RANCE. But my heart and life are one.

CHRIS-TIAN. Who told you that your heart and life were one?

IG-NO-RANCE. My heart tells me so.

CHRIS-TIAN. Your heart tells you so! Lest the Word of God tell you so, all spare proof is of no value.

IG-NO-RANCE. But a good heart has good thoughts and a good life is lived by God's Law.

CHRIS-TIAN. Yes, but it is one thing to have both of these, but it is not the same to just think so.

IG-NO-RANCE. When do our thoughts of our selves come in line with the Word of God?

CHRIS-TIAN. When we judge what the Word of God says of us to be true of our selves. The Word of God says of men when they are born: There is none good, there is none who does good; and it says, The heart and mind of men are vile all the time; and, Man's heart is bad from his youth.

IG-NO-RANCE. I do not think my heart is thus bad, nor ere will.

CHRIS-TIAN. 'Cause you think this way, you have not had one right thought of your self in your life. Tell me, what think you of Christ?

IG-NO-RANCE. I have faith that Christ died for sin and that I will be right with God 'cause I do good and keep his laws. Thus Christ makes my good deeds, good to His Fa-ther, and I will by this be made right.

CHRIS-TIAN. Let me speak to this your faith. The type of faith you speak of is not found at all in the Word of God. Your faith makes Christ a tool to set right not you, but your deeds; and you set right 'cause of your deeds, thus this faith you speak of is false.

IG-NO-RANCE. What! Would you have us trust to what Christ has done with out our deeds? This would cause men to live as they please, with out check or curb.

CHRIS-TIAN. Ig-no-rance is your name, and so you are. You know not what true faith in Christ is.

IG-NO-RANCE. My faith is as good as yours, nor have I the thoughts of fools in my head as you do.

CHRIS-TIAN. Wake up poor Ig-no-rance and see your sins and fly to the Lord Je-sus who is the One who can save you from the wrath to come.

IG-NO-RANCE. You go too fast, I can not keep up with you. Do go on in front of me.

So Chris-tian and Hope-ful out went him and Ig-no-rance came on in back of them. Then Chris-tian said to Hope-ful, I am sad for this poor man. It is sure to go ill with him at the last. Thus they did talk as went on.

Now I saw in my dream that by this time Chris-tian and Hope-ful had got through The En-chant-ed Ground, and had come to the land of Beu-lah, where the air is sweet; and as their Way lay through this land, they did stop here to rest for a while; for here they heard the birds sing, saw the blooms come out on the plants, and the sun shone day and night; it was far past the Val-ley of the Sha-dow of Death, and it was out of the reach of Gi-ant De-spair; nor could they from this place so much as see Doubt-ing Cas-tle.

Now were they in sight of the Ci-ty, and here some of the Bright Ones came to meet them. Here, too, they heard the voice of those who dwelt in the Ci-ty, and had a good view of this land of bliss, which was built of rare gems of all hues, and the streets were laid with gold so that the sun beams which shone on the Ci-ty were too bright for Chris-tian to bear, and he felt sick: and Hope-ful had a fit of the same kind. So they lay by for a time, and wept, for their joy was too much for them.

At length, they walked on their Way, and came near to a place where there were fruit trees, vines, and crops. Now a man stood in the Way, to whom Chris-tian and Hope-ful said: Whose vines and crops are these? He told them they were the King's, and were put there to give joy to those who should go on the road. So he bade them eat what fruit they chose, and took them to see the King's walks; and there they slept.

When they woke, they met two men in clothes that shone like gold, and the face of each shone bright as the light. These men said: Whence come you? And they told them. Then the men said, You have but one thing more to do, which is a hard one, and then you are in the Ce-les-ti-al Ci-ty.

Chris-tian and Hope-ful did then beg of the two men to go with them, which they did. But, they said, it is by your own faith that you must gain it. Then I saw that they went on till they came in sight of the Gate.

Now 'twixt them and the Gate was the Ri-ver of Death which was broad and deep. It had no bridge, and the mere sight of it did so stun Chris-tian and Hope-ful that they could not move.

But the men who went with them said; You can not come to the Gate but through this Riv-er. Is there no way but this one to the Gate? said Chris-tian. Yes, said they, but there have been but two men, to wit, E-noch and E-li-jah, who have trod that path since the world was made.

Then Chris-tian and Hope-ful felt their hearts sink with fear, and gave a look this way and that in much dread of the waves. Yet through it lay the way to Zi-on. Is the Riv-er all of one depth? said Chris-tian. He was told that it was not, yet they could not help them in that case, for he would find the Riv-er more or less deep, as he had faith in the King of the place. So they set foot in the stream, but Chris-tian gave a loud cry to his good friend Hope-ful, and said: The waves close round my head, and I sink. Then said Hope-ful: Be of good cheer; my feet feel the bed of the Riv-er, and it is good.

But Chris-tian said: Ah, Hope-ful, the pains of death have got hold of me; I shall not reach the Ce-les-ti-al Ci-ty that I long for. And with that great dark with fear of heart and dread of mind fell on Chris-tian, so that he could not see.

Hope-ful had much to do to keep Chris-tian's head out of the stream; nay, at times he had quite sunk, and then in a while he would rise up half dead. Then said Hope-ful: I see the Gate, and the men who stand by it to wait for us.

CHRIS-TIAN. It is you they wait for; you have been full of hope since I met you.

HOPE-FUL. And so have you. My friend, all this is sent to try you to see if you will call to mind all that God has done for you, and live on Him in this time of need.

At these words Hope-ful saw that Chris-tian was in deep thought; so he said to him; Be of good cheer, Christ will make thee whole. Then Chris-tian broke out with a loud voice: Oh, I see Him! And He speaks to me and says: When you pass through the deep streams, I will be with you.

And now they both got strength, and the Riv-er was as still as a stone, so that Chris-tian felt the bed of it with his feet, and he could walk through it. Thus they got to the right bank, where the two men in bright robes stood to wait for them.

Now you must bear in mind that Zi-on was on a steep hill, yet did Chris-tian and Hope-ful go up with ease and great speed, for they had these two men to lead them by the arms and 'cause they had left the clothes of their stay on earth* back in the Riv-er of Death.

* their bodies of flesh

The hill stood in the sky, for the base of it was there. So in sweet talk they went up through the air. The Bright Ones told them of the bliss of the place, which they said was such as no tongue could tell, and that there they would see the Tree of Life, and eat of the fruits of it.

When you come there, said they, white robes will be put on you, and your talk from day to day shall be with the King for all time. There you shall not see such things as you saw on earth, to wit, care and want, and woe and death. You now go to be with A-bra-ham, I-saac, and Ja-cob.

CHRIS-TIAN and HOPE-FUL. What must we do there?

They said: You will have rest for all your toil, and joy for all your grief. You will reap what you have sown—the fruit of all the tears you shed for the King by the Way. In that place you will wear crowns of gold, and have at all times a sight of Him who sits on the throne and you shall see Him as He is. And you shall serve Him with praise, shouts of joy, and thanks. You shall both see with your eyes and hear with your ears the Strong One. There too you shall see your friends whom you knew on earth who loved God. And when He shall come back with Sound of Trump, as on the Wings of the Wind, you shall come with Him, and you shall for all time to come, be with the Lord. And when the time comes to judge the world, you shall sit on the Throne of Judg-ment with Him to judge both An-gels and men.

Now, while they thus drew up to the Gate, lo, a host of saints came to meet them, to whom the two Bright Ones said: These are men who loved our Lord when they were in the world, and left all for His name; and He sent us to bring them far on their Way, that they might go in and look on their Lord with joy. Then the whole host with great shouts came round on all sides (as it were to guard them); so that it did seem to Chris-tian and Hope-ful as if all Zi-on had come down to meet them.

Now the Ci-ty it self came to their sight and they thought they heard all the bells in it ring to greet them. Their minds were filled with warm thoughts of joy to think that they would dwell with An-gels, Pro-phets, and Pil-grims like they and would do so for all time.

Then they came up to the Gate and saw on top of it in gold, these words: Blest are they that do His Laws, that they may have the right to The Tree of Life, and may come in through the Gates to the Ci-ty.

Then I saw in my dream, that the Bright Ones told them to call at the Gate. When they did, E-noch, Mo-ses, and E-li-jah did look down on them, to whom it was said, These men are come from the Ci-ty of De-struc-tion for the love they bear to the King of this place. Then Chris-tian and Hope-ful did each hand in their scrolls which they got at the Cross, and the scrolls were brought in to the King, who when He had read them, bid the Gates be flung back for the men to pass in.

Now, when Chris-tian and Hope-ful went in at the Gate a great change took place in them, and they were clad in robes that shone like gold. There were bright hosts that came with

THE GATES ARE OPENED

harps and crowns, and they said to them; Come ye in to the joy of our Lord. And then I heard all the bells in Zi-on ring.

Now just as the Gates were flung back for the men to pass in, I had a sight of the Ci-ty, which shone like the sun; the streets were paved with gold, and those who dwelt there had crowns on their heads, and palms in their hands, and with one voice they sent forth shouts of praise. But the Gates were now once more shut, and I could but wish that I, too, had gone in to share this bliss.

Now as I gazed on these things, I did turn my head to look back, and saw Ig-no-rance come up to the side of the Riv-er, but he soon got through it, for there was in that place a man with a boat named Vain-Hope* that, with his boat, did help Ig-no-rance to cross to the side of the Riv-er where the Ci-ty was.

And I saw Ig-no-rance come up the hill to the Gate, but he came by him self, and no one did cheer him on. When he got up to the Gate he did knock, sure that he would be let in with all speed.

The men came to the top of the Gate and did look down at Ig-no-rance and ask, Where are you from and what would you have? He said, I have ate and drank with the King, and He taught in our streets. They then did ask him for his scroll that they might show it to the King; so he groped for it in his clothes, and found none. Then they said, Have you none? but he spoke not a word.

So they told the King, but He would not come down to see him, but told the Bright Ones that had brought Chris-tian and Hope-ful to the Ci-ty, to go out and take Ig-no-rance and bind him hand and foot, and take him to his own place. So they took him up through the air to the door I had seen in the side of the hill, and put him in there. Then I saw that there was a Way to Hell from the Gates of Hea-ven, as well as from the Ci-ty of De-struc-tion. Then I woke, and lo, it was a dream.

---

* Vain-Hope is the ferry-man who easily guides Ignorance across the River of Death. Such is the death of a self-righteous man who falsely believes that his heart is right with God. Many today approach the River of Death with Vain-Hope as their guide, trusting in a decision they have made or a prayer they have prayed to gain them access to the Celestial City, but their hearts and lives have never been changed by the power of God. Thus like Ignorance, they find when they die, that their profession of faith has been to them but a By-Way to Hell.